You Hold The Reins

Dominion Is Yours

PUBLICATION

OTHER WORKS BY THE SAME AUTHOR. . .

Living Free
Miracles Don't Just Happen
Demons The Answer Book
Run With The Vision
Ecstasy
Cup Of Life
The Face Of Jesus
The True Story Of Clarita Villanueva
Destroying Your Deadliest Enemy
Seven Ways Jesus Healed The People
JIHAD The Holy War

For Additional Information And Your Free Catalog
Write Today To:

Box 12, Dept. B
South Bend, IN 46624

You Hold The Reins
Dominion Is Yours

by

DR. LESTER SUMRALL

President, Lester Sumrall Evangelistic Association, Inc.

You Hold The Reins
Dominion Is Yours

All Scripture quotations are from the King James Version of the Bible.

ISBN 0-937580-26-0

DEDICATION

*This volume is lovingly and sincerely
dedicated to those millions of
Hurt, Humiliated, Harassed, Haunted
Humans of my generation. . .
who have not as yet discovered
the Push, the Power, the Purpose
found in the
Regenerated, Redeemed, Released
disciples of our Lord Jesus Christ.
May you HAVE DOMINION TODAY!*

CONTENTS

INTRODUCTION

Mathematics has its authority--its rules, formulas, and equations.

Music has its authority--its rules of harmony, time, and progression.

Christianity, too, possesses unique authority.

In this book, I present a study relative to the dominion belonging to the born-again person--to the true believer living in divine harmony with Jesus Christ.

And in this study I seek to show how man received dominion--how man lost dominion--and how any child of God can *regain it* and *retain it!*

Dr. Lester Sumrall

Chapter 1

DIVINELY DESIGNED
FOR DOMINION

POWERFUL!

What an energetic word.

SUPREME!

What an elevating word.

God's people are *powerful* and through their power they have a *supreme* relationship to this world.

The Psalmist David reveals man's lofty position and purpose as designed and decreed by his Creator:

> *What is man, that thou art mindful of him?*
> *and the son of man, that thou visitest him?*
> *For thou hast made him a little lower than*
> *the angels and hast crowned him with glory*
> *and honour.*
>
> -- Psalm 8:4,5 KJV

The word translated "angels" in the Authorized King James Version of the Bible is not the Hebrew

11

word for angels. Most good concordances and reference books will confirm that the Hebrew word of the original manuscripts is the word "elohim." Elohim means God. Elohim is the word used for God in Genesis 1:1. *"In the beginning Elohim created the heaven and the earth."*

God created man just a little lower than Himself! In fact, He created man in His own image (Genesis 1:26-28).

King David declared that we are a creation *"a little lower than God."* God is not limited to time, to space, or to energy. This also will be the final state of the redeemed.

God crowned man with glory and honor.

He made man to possess dominion over His creation. God put all the works of His hands under man's feet.

> *Thou madest him to have dominion over the works of thy hands; thou hast put all things under his feet: All sheep and oxen, yea, and the beasts of the field; The fowl of the air, and the fish of the sea, and whatsoever passeth through the paths of the seas.*
>
> -- Psalm 8:6-8

Creatures of the air, land, and sea were placed under the supervision of man.

Just as fish were created to swim, dogs were created to hunt, and worms were created to crawl, so man was created to rule.

Even the Fall did not blot out man's original design for dominion. Through the centuries since creation, men have craved to fulfill their created purpose.

Three Hindrances to Dominion

Adam sinned against his Creator and delivered his dominion into the hands of God's enemy. But through God's great plan of redemption, the Lord Jesus Christ has restored that dominion to those who will receive it.

Today, only a few elements can keep man from entering into his rightful realm of dominion.

Ignorance is the first of those hindering elements. What a person does not know he has, he cannot possess. One could be willed an estate of a million dollars, yet if he never learned of the will he could die a pauper.

Unbelief is an element which can keep a person from entering this divinely appointed position of dominion.

The Holy Spirit through the writer of Hebrews declared that the children of Israel did not enter God's promised land of provision *"because of unbelief"* (Hebrews 3:19). Then He admonished us to be careful lest we come short of entering God's provision for us for the same reason (Hebrews 4).

Dominion is part of that provision. But when a

man or woman cannot trust the promises of God, standing spiritually and emotionally upon what God has said, it is impossible to possess true dominion.

Sin is the greatest element to destroy man's position of dominion. When a person transgresses he lowers himself from the limits and privileges which God ordained for man beginning in the Garden of Eden.

It is essential for a person to be cleansed by the blood of Jesus and to remain clean to exercise dominion.

The Spirit of Might

The Lord Jesus told His disciples that upon His return to heaven, the works that He did they would do.

> *Verily, verily, I say unto you, He that believeth on me, the works that I do shall he do also; and greater works than these shall he do; because I go unto my Father.*
> *-- John 14:12*

It is impossible to do the works of Jesus without *"the spirit of MIGHT."*

Isaiah prophesied before the coming of the Lord Jesus that the spirit of MIGHT would rest upon Him.

And the spirit of the LORD shall rest upon

> *him, the spirit of wisdom and understand-*
> *ing, THE SPIRIT OF counsel and MIGHT,*
> *the spirit of knowledge and of the fear of*
> *the LORD.*
>
> -- Isaiah 11:2

God wants to give every believer the spirit of MIGHT so that our very appearance everywhere we go reveals strength. He wants our presence to be as the Lord Jesus' presence. When Jesus confronted demons they instantly trembled and begged to be let alone.

The Apostle Paul prayed for the believers at Colosse that they might be *"fruitful in every good work...Strengthened with all MIGHT, according to his (God's) glorious POWER"* (Colossians 1:10,11).

I am praying for you as I write this book. I am asking God that in this volume faith will flow through to you and that God will give you THE SPIRIT OF MIGHT.

What you must realize is that there never was a Goliath capable of standing up before any of God's Davids. The devil cannot create an image of strength which God's people cannot destroy.

Jesus said, *"I will build my church; and the gates of hell shall not prevail against it"* (Matthew 16:18).

For a total victory of His eternal Church, we must say of Christ's followers: Every man is a king! Every woman is a queen!

The Bible says, *"NOW are we the sons of God"*

(1 John 3:2). We must act like sons of the Most High!
Now!

Recently in prayer, the Lord spoke to me saying,
"Do you have dominion?"

I replied, "Yes, Lord."

"Then LOOK like it!"

Our appearance must not be sad, depressed, or
defeated.

Again the Lord said, "Do you have dominion?"

I replied, "Yes, Lord."

He said, "Then TALK like it!"

Our speech reveals either dominion or defeat.
Again the Lord asked, "Do you have dominion?"

I replied, "Yes, Lord."

"Then WALK like it!"

Our shoulders must always be high. Our walk must
always be the victory step!

Chapter 2

DOMINION: GIVEN, LOST, REGAINED

Today millions of human beings live in spiritual, mental, and physical bondage. Their number increases fearfully every day.

As never before in history, tremendous and insidious forces seek to degrade human dignity. Untold millions of men and women are held in invisible chains. They are bound by fear, by various evil tormenting habits, and by terrible diseases which crush them. Countless numbers are bound by demon powers.

In primitive lands, all manner of base superstitions make the individual a slave. He is afraid by day and by night of unseen enemies. His religion of demon worship, witchcraft, or spiritism teaches him to fear.

In modern society and the western world, it is oppression and depression that torment millions of people and hold them captive.

Why?

Why is mankind enmeshed in this terrible bondage?

To find the answer, one must go directly to the account of the creation and fall of man as recorded in the Word of God.

Created to Rule

> *And God said, Let us make man in our image, after our likeness: and let them have DOMINION over the fish of the sea, and over the fowl of the air, and over the cattle, and over all the earth, and over every creeping thing that creepeth upon the earth.*
>
> *So God created man in his own image, in the image of God created he him; male and female created he them.*
>
> *And God blessed them, and God said unto them, Be fruitful, and multiply, and replenish the earth, and SUBDUE it: and have DOMINION over the fish of the sea, and over the fowl of the air, and over every living thing that moveth upon the earth.*
>
> -- Genesis 1:26-28

Here God revealed that man was a created being made in His image and after His likeness.

God's love toward Adam is indicated in these words, *"God blessed them."*

His desire for man is indicated in this statement, *"Be fruitful and multiply."*

Man's position on this earth was forever settled when God said, *"Subdue the earth and have dominion over every living thing that liveth upon the earth."*

This was man's beginning and position with God as recorded in the Book of Beginnings.

The great prophet David confirmed this truth.

> *Thou madest him to have DOMINION over the works of thy hands: thou hast put all things under his feet.*
>
> -- Psalm 8:6

The New Testament further substantiated David's prophetic Psalm and man's glorious beginning.

> *But one in a certain place testified, saying, What is man, that thou art mindful of him? or the son of man, that thou visitest him?*
>
> *Thou madest him a little lower than the angels; thou crownedst him with glory and honour, and didst set him over the works of thy hands:*
>
> *Thou hast put all things in subjection under his feet. For in that he put all in subjection under him, he left nothing that is not put under him. . .*
>
> -- Hebrews 2:6-8

19

Fall From Glory

With such an illustrious beginning and possessing credentials of rulership from the Most High, how could man have fallen into the very quagmire of degradation to wear the devil's chains of slavery?

How did man lose his place of dominion, lordship, and sovereignty?

Only the Bible supplies the answer. God's Word declares that man knowledgeably, willfully, and deliberately lost his freedom and became the devil's slave.

In the first place, Adam did not exercise his responsibility of lordship over the garden.

> *And the Lord God took the man, and put him into the garden of Eden to dress it and to KEEP it.*   --Genesis 2:15

The Hebrew word translated "keep" here does not mean keep as we use that word today. For instance, it does not mean keep as we would use it in this way: The Browns will keep our dog while we are on vacation.

This Hebrew word is more nearly like our word "guard ." You can see that from the next time this word is used in the Bible.

> *So he drove out the man; and he placed at the east of the garden of Eden Cherubims, and a flaming sword which turned*

*every way to KEEP the way of the tree of
life.*

-- Genesis 3:24

Adam was to guard the garden. He must have
known there was an enemy of God from which to
guard it.

He had been given dominion over every thing that
moved. The serpent moved.

He was not deceived (1 Timothy 2:14). He know-
ingly sinned against God and delivered his kingdom
and place of leadership on the earth into the hands of
God's enemy (Luke 4:6).

On the same day Adam transgressed against God,
he died spiritually. Fear was born in his heart. He hid
himself from God among the trees because he was a-
fraid. That day physical mortification began and
Adam began to die physically.

The spirit of man fell and he was separated from
God, the Great Spirit. The highest part of his com-
plex being had lost dominion. He was now wearing
the devil's chains of slavery.

What a change! With great dignity Adam had worn
his vested authority. He was created to rule. But man
either has dominion—or he is under dominion. He
cannot be neutral. Man was created to be dominated
by no force except the Divine. He was created to be
conqueror over any power or influence before him.
When this divinely-set order is not in force, the result
is disaster.

When man fell he caused the entire world--his kingdom--to fall with him. First John 5:19 declares that *"the whole world lieth in darkness."*

Utter chaos was ushered into creation by *"the prince of this world," "the prince of darkness,"* the evil *"god of this world,"* the devil. (See John 12:31, 16:11; Ephesians 6:12; 2 Corinthians 4:4.)

The very animals Adam had named no longer obeyed him. And a lamb could not dwell with the wolf.

Threefold Fall

Man fell from God's grace into sin. He did not stumble or slip; he fell into the very gutters of disgrace, dispair, and disease.

His fall was threefold (Genesis 3:6):

1. BODY. He *looked* upon the fruit of the tree of the knowledge of good and evil. He *saw* that the tree was good for food. So he *lusted* for that food. First John 2:16 says, *"For all that is in the world, the lust of the flesh, and the lust of the eyes, and the pride of life, is not of the Father, but is of the world."* This was the first instance of lust of the flesh.

2. SOUL. The fruit was *pleasant* to the eyes. Adams's soul *desired* this forbidden fruit. This unholy desire meant rebellion against God. By not controlling his eyes and looking to the Lord who created

him, he *permitted* his eyes to lust for the forbidden. This caused his downfall.

3. SPIRIT. He was told the fruit would make him *wise*. This was the sin of the spirit or, *"the pride of life."*

Man fell completely--body, soul, and spirit. In doing so, he instantly lost his lordship, his dominion over evil and disease.

Rule Regained

At this terrible collapse of man, God immediately initiated His plan--His glorious plan of redemption to redeem man from his fallen state.

He promised a Redeemer born of a virgin who would bruise Satan's head.

> *And I will put enmity between thee and the woman, and between thy seed and her seed; it shall bruise thy head, and thou shalt bruise his heel.*
>
> -- Genesis 3:15

Love impelled Him. Love was the purpose for the dispensations He set up from Adam to Calvary.

Ultimately, God made the master stroke! He sent His only begotten Son, the Lord Jesus Christ to pay the penalty for man's sin--and to utterly defeat the devil for man, bringing man back into a place of divine dominion.

The Bible tells us we are to be giving thanks unto the Father for His wonderful plan which *already* has taken us from Satan's hand.

> *Giving thanks unto the Father, which hath made us meet to be partakers of the inheritance of the saints in light:*
>
> *WHO HATH DELIVERED US from the power of darkness and HATH TRANSLATED US into the kingdom of his dear Son:*
>
> *In whom WE HAVE REDEMPTION, through his blood, even the forgiveness of sins:*
>
> -- Colossians 1:12-14

Chapter 3

CHRIST
AND DOMINION

No person who ever walked the face of this earth so asserted dominion as the Lord Jesus Christ.

He knew Divine dominion. *"For in him dwelleth all the fulness of the Godhead bodily"* (Colossians 2:9).

Christ's Miraculous Birth

Our Lord Jesus had dominion in every stage of his life.

His virgin birth, first spoken of in the Garden of Eden, had been prophesied through the prophet Isaiah 750 years before the Babe lay in the manger.

> *Therefore the Lord himself shall give you a sign; Behold, a virgin shall conceive, and bear a son, and shall call his name Immanuel.*
> -- Isaiah 7:14

His supernatural birth transgressed the laws of nature (Luke 1:13-35).

> *And the angel answered and said unto her,*
> *The Holy Ghost shall come upon thee, and*
> *the power of the Highest shall overshadow*
> *thee: therefore also that holy thing which*
> *shall be born of thee shall be called the Son*
> *of God.*
>
>   -- Luke 1:35

The One who had lived through all Eternity--the One who was with God and was God--the One by whom all things were made--became flesh and dwelt among us (John 1:1-4,14).

Through the power of the Holy Ghost He entered the body prepared for Him so that He might defeat Satan for us.

> *Wherefore when he cometh into the*
> *world, he saith, Sacrifice and offering*
> *thou wouldest not, but a body hast thou*
> *prepared me:*
> *In burnt offerings and sacrifices for*
> *sin thou hast had no pleasure.*
> *Then said I, Lo, I come (in the volume*
> *of the book it is written of me,) to do thy*
> *will, O God.*
>
>   -- Hebrews 10:5-7

His supernatural entry into the world set the stage for a life of total dominion.

Youth and Dominion

At twelve years of age the Lord showed amazing force for power as He not only asked questions of the shrewd lawyers in Jerusalem, but He answered their questions.

> *And it came to pass, that after three days they found him in the temple, sitting in the midst of the doctors, both hearing them, and asking them questions.*
> *And all that heard him were astonished at his understanding and answers.*
> -- Luke 2:46,47

The strength of His eyes and words brought *astonishment* to the intellectuals of Jerusalem.

Temptation and Dominion

Immediately after Jesus was baptized of John in the Jordan--and immediately after the Spirit of God descended upon Him like a dove, and the Father from heaven said, *"This is my beloved Son, in whom I am well pleased"*--Jesus went forth into the wilderness to exercise dominion over the temptations of the devil.

He met temptations of the spirit, temptations of the soul, and temptations of the body while living in a body of flesh. He defeated them all with the power of the written word of God and the word of His testimony.

"It is written," He powerfully declared, *"man shall not live by bread alone, but by every word that proceedeth out of the mouth of God"* Matthew 4:4).

His First Miracle

At the beginning of Christ's public ministry, His first miracle was the turning of spring water into sparkling delicious wine (John 2:1-11). This was accomplished without the fermentation process of nature.

> *This beginning of miracles did Jesus in Cana of Galilee, and manifested forth his glory; and his disciples believed on him.*
> -- John 2:11

Those around Him were suddenly aware of His dominion. They beheld nature obey Him!

Teacher With Authority

Jesus went about teaching. But His teaching was like none the people ever had heard--and they recognized a difference immediately. What made it different?

> *And it came to pass, when Jesus had ended these sayings, the people were astonished at his doctrine: For he taught them as one having AUTHORITY, and not as the scribes.*
>
> -- Matthew 7:28,29

The *authority* in His teaching marked the difference!

Dominion Over Thieves and Tradition

The spirit of MIGHT was upon Him! And everyone stood back and watched while He worked.

> *And Jesus went into the temple of God, and cast out all them that sold and bought in the temple, and overthrew the tables of the moneychangers, and the seats of them that sold doves, And said unto them, IT IS WRITTEN, My house shall be called the house of prayer; but ye have made it a den of thieves.*
>
> *And the blind and the lame came to him in the temple; and he healed them.*
>
> *And when the chief priests and scribes saw the wonderful things that he did, and*

> *the children crying in the temple saying,*
> *Hosanna to the son of David; they were*
> *sore displeased.*
>
> -- Matthew 21:12-15

Tradition is a terrible power. Tradition is a killing influence. Tradition is a rut, a grave--it can bury you. You can get down so deeply into tradition as to say, "It's always been done that way and we are always going to do it that way." God has no opportunity to move in a new way to help and bless you or to set you free.

Notice that when Jesus had loosed the temple of God from men's traditions that the blind and the lame came to Him and He healed them.

Dominion Over Nature

> *And in the fourth watch of the night Jesus*
> *went unto them, walking on the sea. And*
> *when the disciples saw him walking on the*
> *sea, they were troubled. . . .*
>
> -- Matthew 14:25,26

Christ showed Himself to be the master of nature by walking upon the Sea of Galilee. His disciples were troubled and amazed at such dominion.

He further demonstrated His power over nature by calming the tempestuous sea with a spoken word.

And there arose a great storm of wind, and the waves beat into the ship, so that it was now full. And he was in the hinder part of the ship, asleep on a pillow: and they awake him, and say unto him, Master, carest thou not that we perish?

And he arose, and rebuked the wind, and said unto the sea, Peace, be still. And the wind ceased, and there was a great calm.

And he said unto them, Why are ye so fearful? how is it that ye have no faith?

And they feared exceedingly, and said one to another, What manner of man is this, that even the wind and the sea obey him?

-- Mark 4:37-41

Devastating upheaval occurred in the perfect weather system Adam knew and enjoyed when Satan entered the scene. Since that hour, storms and winds have driven man who was created to rule the world into holes in the ground.

Jesus rebuked the storm. He spoke to the sea. And they obeyed His words.

What's more, He rebuked His disciples for being fearful and faithless.

Dominion Over Disease and Sickness

How God anointed Jesus of Nazareth with

31

> *the Holy Ghost and with power: who went about doing good, and healing all that were oppressed of the devil; for God was with him.*
>
> -- Acts 10:38

Throughout His earthwalk Jesus went about doing good and healing. He exercised complete dominion over the disease and sickness Satan had brought to mankind.

A Roman centurion--a man who understood authority--recognized Jesus' authority and caused the Master to marvel at the centurion's faith.

The centurion came to Jesus on behalf of his servant who was at home, grievously tormented of the palsy. When Jesus said, *"I will come and heal him,"* the centurion answered:

> *Lord, I am not worthy that thou shouldest come under my roof: but SPEAK THE WORD ONLY, and my servant shall be healed.*
>
> *For I am a man under authority, having soldiers under me: and I say to this man, Go, and he goeth; and to another, Come, and he cometh; and to my servant, Do this, and he doeth it.*
>
> *When Jesus heard it, he marvelled, and said unto them that followed, Verily I say unto you, I have not found so great faith,*

no, not in Israel. . .

And Jesus said unto the centurion, Go thy way; and as thou hast believed, so be it done unto thee. And his servant was healed in the selfsame hour.

-- Matthew 8:8-10,13

Christ healed that servant with the spoken word of authority.

Recognizing that authority and placing faith in it drew a commendation for the Roman officer just as not recognizing it in faith drew a rebuke for the disciples in the ship.

Many scriptures reveal that throughout His ministry He always exercised authority over sickness and disease. He never failed to heal those who were brought to Him.

When the even was come, they brought unto him many that were possessed with devils: and he cast out the spirits with his word, and healed all that were sick.

-- Matthew 8:16

The Lord Jesus never revealed any fear from nature nor from disease. He dominated them completely.

Dominion Over Death

In at least three cases the Lord Jesus asserted His

dominion over the powers of death by raising the dead.

He raised a girl from the dead (Mark 5).

He raised a boy from the dead (Luke 7:11-15).

He raised a man, Lazarus, from the dead (John 11).

The girl He raised from the dead was still in her home.

The boy was on his funeral bier which was at the cemetery gate on its way to the cemetery.

The man was already in his tomb. Lazarus had been dead four days.

Christ possessed dominion over death.

Dominion Over Devils

From the beginning of His ministry the Lord Jesus demonstrated His power over evil spirits of all kinds.

The following is only one of several such cases the Bible records. I use it because it includes in one case several points I wish to make. 1) Demons recognized Him and feared Him. 2) Sometimes they raged against their victims in a final effort to remain, but the words of faith from the mouth of the Lord Jesus always caused them to come forth and the person to be set free. 3) People could see His authority and power.

And in the synagogue there was a man, which had a spirit of an unclean devil, and cried out with a loud voice, Saying, Let us alone; what have we to do with thee, thou

Jesus of Nazareth? art thou come to destroy us? I know thee who thou art; the Holy One of God.

And Jesus rebuked him, saying, Hold thy peace, and come out of him. And when the devil had thrown him in the midst, he came out of him, and hurt him not.

And they were all amazed, and spake among themselves, saying, WHAT A WORD IS THIS! for with AUTHORITY and POWER he commandeth the unclean spirits, and they come out.

-- Luke 4:33-36

The demoniac of Gadara had 2000 or more such demons. Mary Magdalene had seven.

Some had spirits of blindness, some spirits of dumbness, some unclean spirits, but they all yielded to His dominion.

No person on record has so revealed and taught dominion as the Lord Jesus. The Bible says of Him, *"In whom are hid all the treasures of wisdom and knowledge"* (Colossians 2:3).

Dominion in
Death, Burial, and Resurrection

The Apostle Paul called the demonic powers in the world system *"princes of this world, that come to nought"* (1 Corinthians 2:6).

Then he spoke of the glorious plan of God that brought them to nought.

> *But we speak the wisdom of God in a*
> *mystery, even the hidden wisdom, which*
> *God ordained before the world unto our*
> *glory:*
> *Which none of the princes of this world*
> *knew: for had they known it, they would*
> *not have crucified the Lord of glory.*
> *-- 1 Corinthians 2:7,8*

The devil and his cohorts played right into the plan of God and their own doom when they took part in offering the Supreme Sacrifice for the sins of man.

In His death, burial, and resurrection, Jesus completely destroyed the power of the enemy and delivered mankind.

> *Forasmuch then as the children are par-*
> *takers of flesh and blood, he also himself*
> *likewise took part of the same; that*
> *through death he might destroy him that*
> *had the power of death, that is, the devil;*
> *And deliver them who through fear of*
> *death were all their lifetime subject to*
> *bondage.*
> *-- Hebrews 2:14,15*

> *Buried with him in baptism, wherein*

also ye are risen with him through the faith of the operation of God, who hath raised him from the dead.

And you. . .hath he quickened together with him, having forgiven you all trespasses;

Blotting out the handwriting of ordinances that was against us, which was contrary to us, and took it out of the way, nailing it to his cross;

And having spoiled principalities and powers, he made a shew of them openly, triumphing over them in it.

-- Colossians 2:12-15

How we can cry with Paul, *"That I may know Him, and the power of His resurrection!"* (Philippians 3:10).

When Jesus appeared to John the Revelator on the Isle of Patmos, He said, *"I am He that liveth, and was dead; and,behold, I am alive for evermore. And I have the keys of hell and of death"* (Revelation 1:18).

Keys represent authority.

Supreme Dominion

After His resurrection--and then after walking forty days with His followers--Jesus concluded His earthly ministry by declaring, *"All power is given unto me in heaven and in earth...."* (Matthew 28:18).

37

That is supreme dominion!

But notice this--Jesus did not stop there. He went on to say, *"All power is given unto me in heaven and in earth, GO YE THEREFORE...."*

Jesus delegated the authority on the earth to His body, the Church.

Mark's account of this momentous delegation of authority declares that He said, *"And these signs shall follow them that believe; IN MY NAME, shall they cast out devils; they shall speak with new tongues; They shall take up serpents; and if they drink any deadly thing, it shall not hurt them; they shall lay hands on the sick, and they shall recover"* (Mark 16:17,18).

Dominion over the devil, demons, sickness, disease, and all the power of the enemy is now restored to His body, the Church, IN HIS NAME!

Chapter 4

WHAT IS HUMAN DOMINION?

The scope of dominion is so great, we must have a clear definition of what dominion is. We must learn its laws, know its source and its limitations.

The word dominion is from a Greek word *kurios* which in New Testament usage means lordship, inherited rulership, sovereignty.

When we refer to human dominion it immediately speaks to us of struggle. Human dominion is not automatic. Dominion is an achievement.

Mortals on the face of this earth reach for dominion. This is true from the cowboy who subdues a wild horse and knows a burst of strength and rulership to the stockmarket broker who discovers a bonanza in the market.

Dominate or Be Dominated

Every human will know either dominion or slavery.

The reason for this is that man's enemy, the devil, seeks to enslave him and will never cease in his efforts.

Jesus Christ already has paid the full price for man's redemption from the hands of this relentless foe. He cries to the world, *"If the Son therefore shall make you free, ye shall be free indeed"* (John 8:36).

It is true that one man lost the dominion God had given mankind. But it is also true that one Man regained the reign.

> *For if by one man's offense death reigned by one; MUCH MORE they which receive abundance of grace and of the gift of righteousness SHALL REIGN IN LIFE by one, Jesus Christ.*
>
> -- Romans 5:17

The *Amplified* translation reveals that the fuller meaning of the Greek is *"shall reign as kings in life."*

If you are in Jesus Christ the right to reign as a king in life is yours. Don't allow the devil to dominate you--you dominate him!

If you are not yet in the royal family of God, take this moment to accept Jesus as your Savior and Lord and be born into the ruling class right now. Romans 10:9,10 tells you how to be born again.

Human Dominion in Three Realms

Dominion awaits man in three great areas. They are

the areas of his makeup: spirit, soul, and body.

> *Abstain from all appearance of evil. And*
> *the very God of peace sanctify you wholly;*
> *and I pray God your whole spirit and soul*
> *and body be preserved blameless unto the*
> *coming of our Lord Jesus Christ.*
>   -- 1 Thessalonians 5:22,23

Man is a trinity.

God made man a spirit. God is a Spirit (John 4:24). And man is made in the image of God.

Man possesses a soul and a body.

God made man's spirit to be king of his triune personality, with the soul and body under obedience.

To define these three areas of man we will begin with the most easily identified--*the body*. God fashioned a human body from the clay of the earth (Genesis 2:7). There was to be a close kindred between man and his environment. His outer shell would be like the area in which he lives.

The body's five senses are: seeing, tasting, smelling, touching, and hearing. This earthly part of man was created to be a slave to the immortal part of man which is his spirit. If the inward man is evil the carnal clay man will manifest this evil. If the inner man is spiritually alive, the body man demonstrates the fruit of the spirit.

Inside this shell, or clay house, God placed a soul.

The soul is made up of three tremendous areas of being:

Intellect - where man thinks

Emotions - where man feels

Will - where man decides

God created the soul and the body to be subservient to *the spirit* of man. This spirit is as distinct from the other two areas of man as light is from darkness. God gave man's spirit the propensities of communion with Deity. In this area man is able to communicate with the divine world. God gave man in his spirit the structure of intuition and the power of conscience.

Man's spirit contacts God. And God only speaks to man through man's spirit.

Man's soul contacts his fellow men.

Man's body contacts the earth--the physical realm.

Let's look at the first man--Adam. *With his body* he walked, ate, saw, heard, and felt. *With his soul* he possessed the power to name all the animals on the earth. He had the intellect to operate the Garden of Eden as its overseer. He possessed emotions to admire the sunrise and the sunset, to feel affection toward his wife. He had the willpower to choose what he would do as he walked in the Garden as its king. *With his spirit* man walked with God in the evening and conversed with God. With his spirit he understood his limitations, such as the forbidden fruit from the Tree of the Knowledge of Good and Evil.

God made man's spirit to be the king of this triunity. God made man's soul to be the servant to serve and obey the spirit. And the body was made to be a slave to carry out the wishes of the spirit directed by the soul.

As long as Adam lived in the spirit and his being was dominated by his spirit, he had perfect fellowship with God, with his environment, and with himself. He was a whole person. He was well adjusted. He was supremely happy.

But when Adam rebelled and disobeyed God, his spirit died. His actions and thoughts now controlled by his soul and body were each out of relationship with God--and Satan controlled his being.

Spirit Dominion

When a sinner comes to Christ and is born again, the spirit becomes reinstated as king.

The spirit of man must know dominion in order to achieve greatness in faith and greatness in achievement. If the spirit of man does not know dominion, then no portion of his person has hope of rulership.

Daily, the born-again man should seek to achieve strength and power in his spirit.

How?

By feeding his spirit with God's Word (1 Peter 2:2).

By prayer and communication with God.

By praying in tongues. He that speaks in tongues edifies himself--he builds up his spirit (1 Cor. 14:4).

43

By exercising his spirit. By walking in faith.

Soulical Power

There are three separate worlds of action in the soul of man where the devil seeks to enthrone himself.

The mind. God wants the human mind under divine subjection. It should be directed through the human spirit by the Holy Spirit. But the devil, above all, wants to capture the human mind. Because the mind of man is so important, it has been--and is--a perpetual battlefield. The mind suffers greater onslaughts from the power of darkness than any other part of the human personality.

Christians are to renew their minds (Romans 12:2). How? With the Word of God.

We are to bring every thought into captivity to the obedience of Christ (2 Corinthians 10:3-5).

We are to control what our minds think (Philippians 4:8).

The mind, yielded to the human spirit which is yielded to the Holy Spirit, is active! (1 Peter 1:13), powerful! even the mind of Christ! (1 Corinthians 2:16).

Emotions. The deepest depression to the highest exaltation are possible in the gamut of emotions. If man does not dominate his emotions, his life can be one of defeat.

Emotions dominated by a source other than God or the man himself cause stress. Stress, doctors say, is what kills man.

Dominion has to do with relaxing. Relaxing has to do with releasing. Releasing has to do with giving our total being over to God for His care. When our emotions are in the Almighty care of our Lord, stress and struggle have no place in us.

The will. No person can fully know dominion with stubbornness of will. The Bible speaks of those who are self-willed. This means that their natural human nature is in rulership and God's spirit of dominion is defeated and subjected to the smaller nature of man.

Dominion in the Natural World

Man's body is his natural relationship to this earth. God wants our corporate person to have dominion as well as our spirit. He does not want any part of us to be dominated by the devil.

One area, for example, in which the devil seeks to dominate man's relationship to this earth, is in the area of finance and earthly possession.

God wants His sons to prosper and to have an abundance for the work of the kingdom.

A person with dominion in this area knows how to do his job well. He knows how to handle money. His motives are right.

If his motives are selfish, then he is outside the

realm of dominion. He is being dominated.

A person with dominion in this area knows how to treat his fellow man. He rejoices with being at peace with God.

A person living in the humblest of circumstances can enjoy dominion in this realm.

Dominion: Gift of God

God created Adam not like the mountains to be big and hard. God created man not like the flowers to be fragile and easily broken. But God created man to be ruler of this earth.

Since the Garden of Eden, however, the devil has contested man's dominion in every generation. Adam lost his dominion. Noah refused to lose his and became a giant of all times.

Abraham knew his dominion in all three realms: of spirit, when he talked with God; of soul, when he obeyed and walked with God; of body, which through his lineage brought the Savior to the world.

Our Lord Jesus said, *"But if I cast out devils by the Spirit of God, then the kingdom of God is come unto you. Or else how can one enter into a strong man's house, and spoil his goods, except he first bind the strong man? and then he will spoil his house"* (Matthew 12:28,29).

Jesus forever told His followers that dominion over the devil was His. The strong man in this scripture is the devil. Christ has dominion over him. He gives that dominion to us.

Our dominion comes directly from the Lord Jesus Christ as a gift. When we connect with Christ, He is our strength.

You can hold a telephone in your hand and never hear a voice until a connection is made. When you connect, you can talk around the world. I have talked 12,000 miles away in a whisper. Without the connection I could not have been heard in the next room.

It is important to be connected to Jesus. Without His power we can never know dominion.

I can hold a piece of wire in my hand. It can be of very little substance. But as it is connected to voltage, that same wire can carry enough power to kill a man.

Disconnected, the wire is almost useless. But connected it can drive a motor which can move a wheel --it can make money--not of itself, but of the power that runs through it.

When I speak of human dominion, I am not talking about human achievement under human psychology, or the brilliance of the natural mind, or the strength of man. This dominion is the gift of God.

The Indian Boy and the Light Bulb

Several years ago I was doing evangelistic work in the hinder parts of Paraguay. I went up the Paraguay River and then rode horseback through Grand Chaco.

In one of the Indian tribes we met an Indian boy.

He had gone adventuring by the river into a city far from home.

In the evening time he had seen a light shining in a local store. He was fascinated by the bright bulb.

"What is that?" he asked the storekeeper.

"It is used at night to take away darkness."

"Can I buy one?"

The storekeeper sold him a light bulb. It took all the boy's money to buy it.

As the Indian boy journeyed home to his primitive tribe he thought of the wonder it would be to them when they saw this bulb so brilliant at night.

But to his amazement, when he produced the bulb before his people, it would not light up. He tried and tried, but he failed to make it glow.

What he did not know was that behind the store there was a generator making the power to turn on the light. The light in the bulb had to connect with the power from the generator.

A human being's light is like that bulb. He has no light except when he is connected with Jesus Christ who generates power within him.

Human dominion is God's power moving in the total being of the born-again person.

Chapter 5

WHO CAN HAVE DOMINION ?

Is the victorious life of Christian dominion only for the chosen few. . .or, is it for every disciple who receives Christ as Lord and Savior?

I believe the promises of the New Testament are always to any and every true disciple. Jesus Christ said:

> *Behold, I give unto you power to tread on serpents and scorpions, and over all the power of the enemy: and nothing shall by any means hurt you.*
>
> -- Luke 10:19

> *Verily, I say unto you, Whatsoever ye shall bind on earth shall be bound in heaven: and whatsoever ye shall loose on earth shall be loosed in heaven.*
>
> -- Matthew 18:18

In his Epistles to the Church, the Apostle Paul enunciated repeatedly the privileges and blessings which belong to each child of God.

> *Blessed be the God and Father of our Lord Jesus Christ, who hath blessed us with all spiritual blessings in heavenly places in Christ.*
>
> -- Ephesians 1:3

Dominion is for every believer who will accept the responsibility for exerting it.

In discussing the subject of dominion and authority, I most certainly am not dealing with human conceit and bigotry. I am only explaining the divine birthrights as recorded in God's Word. I have observed that the person who possesses true dominion is always a humble servant of the Lord.

Robbed of Rule

After a person is born again, the devil seeks in every way possible to hide the believer's position of authority from him. Satan knows that when the believer is aware of his privileges and power, he (Satan) will be completely defeated and his works destroyed.

An age-long strategy of the devil is to attack the believer in the area of confession. He knows a person never will rise above his confession.

Instead of making the promises of God his confession of faith, the believer constantly confesses his sicknesses, faults, and weaknesses.

Since a man is what he confesses himself to be, the devil uses this means to keep the believer in bondage.

Remember: Satan does not want you to confess dominion in Christ, victories by the blood and by the abundance of God's gift. For when you make these your confession, you exert dominion, authority, and power.

Authorized Dealers

It is my observation that people don't like substitutes.

For this reason, an automobile dealer displays a sign over his business which reads, "Authorized Dealer." The sign means a consumer can expect genuine parts for his car and factory-trained mechanics to install them--and no substitutes.

In the spiritual world, Bible-believing Christians are God's authorized dealers of His dominion. They have what God wants this world to have. It would be most fitting for the Church to put out a sign which says, "Authorized Dealer of God's Spirit and Power."

Perpetual Power

The early Church had power. The known world was shaken by that power Christ had promised.

> *Ye shall receive power, after that the Holy*
> *Ghost is come upon you.*
>
> -- Acts 1:8

That this dominion was to continue after Pentecost is evident. Peter preaching on the day of Pentecost said:

> *For the promise is unto you, and to your*
> *children, and to all that are afar off, even*
> *as many as the Lord our God shall call.*
>
> -- Acts 2:39

These words clearly reveal that this dominion was not only for the apostles. It was for the great mass of people who heard Peter's sermon. It was for their children. And it was for those afar off--even us today.

Repeatedly, the New Testament emphasizes that this divine dominion was not exclusively for the apostles.

> *And Stephen, full of faith and power, did*
> *great wonders and miracles among the*
> *people.*
>
> -- Acts 6:8

Stephen was a deacon in the church of Jerusalem. And the record says he possessed great dominion, so much so that wonders and miracles took place.

> *Then Philip went down to the city of Samaria, and preached Christ unto them.*
>
> *And the people with one accord gave heed unto those things which Philip spake, hearing and seeing the miracles which he did.*
>
> *For unclean spirits, crying with loud voice, came out of many that were possessed with them: and many taken with palsies, and that were lame, were healed.*
>
> *And there was great joy in that city.*
>
> -- Acts 8:5-8

Philip also was a deacon in the church of Jerusalem. And people were healed and set free through his ministry.

I always have encouraged the lay members of the churches I have pastored not only to pray for themselves, but also to pray for others, and to expect answers from God. Many miracles of healing and deliverance have resulted through their prayers.

Clearly, dominion is not for the select few. It is for every disciple of the Lord Jesus Christ.

Chapter 6

THE INSTRUMENTS OF DOMINION

A soldier is never sent into battle until he has a complete understanding of the instruments of his warfare. Until a soldier knows the power of his guns and the range of their effectiveness, he is not capable of victory and routing the enemy.

Until a Christian disciple understands the instruments of his dominion, he cannot effectively use them. The Christian must know what to do and when to do it in order to win the necessary victory.

Jesus Christ has given to His disciples all the instruments necessary for dominion on this earth.

1. THE BIBLE. Without the Bible--man's source Book of Truth--man cannot have dominion.

Possibly the greatest instrument of man's dominion on the face of the earth is the written Word of God. It is the instrument Jesus used to defeat Satan in the wilderness of temptation. He declared, *"IT IS WRIT-TEN. . . ."* And then, *"IT IS WRITTEN AGAIN. . . ."*

And the third time, *"Get thee hence, Satan: FOR IT IS WRITTEN...."* (Matthew 4:4,7,10).

This instrument is our sword (Ephesians 6:17). It is alive, powerful, and sharp (Hebrews 4:12). Like Jesus, we can use this sword with our mouths against the enemy (Matthew 4; Luke 4; Revelation 19:15).

The Bible is infallible. It is inspirational. It is inerrant in its information.

The Bible is supernatural in its application to the human life.

In my personal life the Bible has been a true guide in every crisis. God has directed me through His Word when He wanted me to do something of a different nature. The Bible is my source book for truth. When I wish to know what is right and wrong, I refer myself to what the Bible says about the matter.

No human can have total dominion in his own life-- no person can truly hold the reins and be in control-- without putting the Bible in a prominent position for his life.

The men and women I have met in my travels throughout the world who were truly people of spiritual power were those for whom the Bible was the strongest factor in their spiritual life.

2. THE NAME OF JESUS. Jesus gave His Body --the Church--His Name. The Name of Jesus is above every name. At that Name, beings in heaven, in earth, and under the earth must bow (Philippians 2:9-11). That Name is dominion!

Before He was crucified, Jesus spoke to His follow-

ers of the soon-coming day when He would give them
the power of attorney to use His exalted Name. They
would use it in prayer (John 16:23,24). He spoke of
His followers doing the works that He did, and greater works, because He was going unto His Father. In
the next breath He said, *"Whatsoever ye shall ask IN
MY NAME, that will I do, that the Father may be
glorified in the Son. If ye shall ask any thing IN MY
NAME, I will do it"* (John 14:13,14).

After His death, burial, and resurrection, and before He ascended to sit down at the right hand of
Majesty on High, Jesus gave us the Great Commission, *"Go ye into all the world. . . ."*

The Gospel of Mark records the signs which would
follow the believers as they carried out His orders.
*"IN MY NAME shall they cast out devils. . . they
shall speak with new tongues. . .they shall take up
serpents. . .if they drink any deadly thing, it shall not
hurt them. . .they shall lay hands on the sick, and
they shall recover"* (Mark 16:15-18).

That's dominion! And it's all in His Name!

Every soldier of the cross who walks in victory and
dominion knows that he possesses this mighty weap-
on--and he knows how to use it.

Peter and John did. At the Gate Beautiful they said
to a man who lay there daily, lame from his mother's
womb, *"Such as I have give I thee: IN THE NAME of
Jesus Christ of Nazareth rise up and walk"* (Acts 3).

3. FAITH. Without dynamic faith, born in the
Christian heart at conversion and nourished through

the Word of God, a believer cannot successfully engage in battle with demon power and win.

When Jesus came down from the mount where He was gloriously transfigured, He was met with the news that His disciples had been unable to cast the devil out of a certain man's lunatic son. His first reaction to the report was, *"Oh faithless generation."*

The devil departed, of course, at Jesus' command.

His disciples asked Jesus, *"Why could not we cast him out?"*

"Because of your unbelief," Jesus replied. *"If you have faith as a grain of mustard seed, ye shall say unto this mountain, Remove hence to yonder place; and it shall remove; and nothing shall be impossible unto you"* (Matthew 17:14-20).

When a person is challenged by temptation, or disease, or the devil, his faith must constantly come into focus. He must have faith to command God's power. God explains that He desires we command Him. *"Thus saith the Lord, the Holy One of Israel, and his Maker, Ask me of things to come concerning my sons, and concerning the work of my hands command ye me"* (Isaiah 45:11).

We see this ministry of commanding God exemplified with Abraham, a man the New Testament refers to many times as an example of faith.

God did not hide from Abraham that He was going to destroy Sodom and Gomorrah.

Abraham stood before the Lord and said, *"Wilt thou also destroy the righteous with the wicked?. . .*

*Peradventure there be fifty righteous within the city:
wilt thou also destroy and not spare the place for the
fifty righteous that are therein? That be far from thee
to do after this manner, to slay the righteous with the
wicked:. . .Shall not the Judge of all the earth do
right?"* (Genesis 18:17-25).

How did the Creator react to such words from the
tongue of a man? He agreed to Abraham's demand.
He said He would not destroy those wicked cities for
the sake of fifty.

Abraham decreased the number of the righteous to
forty-five, then forty, then thirty, then twenty, and
finally to ten. Each time the Lord was willing to meet
Abraham's demand.

The true power of faith never has been fully uti-
lized by man. God is still waiting for heroes of faith
to use the divine dominion He gave to Adam in the
Garden of Eden.

In the New Testament Church, it was the force of
faith which caused Peter to turn to the body of a
dead woman and say, *"Tabitha, arise"* (Acts 9:40).
It was by faith that the Apostle Paul commanded the
spirit of divination to come out of the fortune-telling
damsel (Acts 16:18).

Faith is the key which unlocks the generosity and
strength of God.

Faith pleases God. And without faith it is impossible to please Him (Hebrews 11:6).

4.KNOWLEDGE. God's Word says, *"My people
are destroyed for lack of knowledge. . . ."* (Hosea

4:6). Without knowledge of his true relationship with God, man cannot possess dominion over the many conflicts of life.

Suppose someone kidnaps a king's only son, the crown prince of the realm. Later, the child is abandoned. A beggar finds the boy, and having no idea of his identity, out of compassion adopts him. Now the child of the king eats beggar's refuse, clothes himself in filthy rags, and begs from house to house.

But suppose further, that the king knows the young prince by a birthmark which establishes his identity beyond question. The royal father never gives up in his search for the prince. One day the king hears that a child resembling his son lives in a distant city with a beggar. Arriving at the beggar's hovel, the king examines the child and finds him to be his son.

A tremendous change suddenly takes place. The crown prince is washed and groomed. He is given a robe, a ring, and a place of authority over the servants.

My point is that the crown prince, even though he was the son of the king, while living with the beggar was no different from the beggar. He did not know his position of dominion.

Many Christians today are like that. They belong to Christ, they are sons of God, yet the devil keeps them in ignorance so they will not realize their divine right of dominion. For once they understand the basis of their dominion in Christ, they live a new life attendant with power and victories.

It is imperative that you know--and *know* that you know--your rights as a follower of the Lord Jesus Christ. For YOU are entitled to dominion.

5. *PRAYER.* Prayer is one of the most powerful instruments of the disciple. Prayer is actually the council chamber where divine commands are issued. In prayer, the believer receives the solution to his problems. In prayer, he receives the infilling of divine energy. Jesus revealed this when He prayed and fasted for forty days and then met Satan single-handedly in the greatest spiritual struggle recorded in history.

Every outstanding person of God in history has been a person of prayer. It is not possible to possess great dominion and not constantly return to the Master to receive instructions from Him.

Prayer is power--power as real as terrestrial gravity.

Elijah demonstrated the dominion of prayer when he called upon God to send rain upon the land. The New Testament specifically points out that Elijah was a man, as we are. The difference is, he knew how to pray.

The early Church prayed and the place where they were assembled together was shaken (Acts 4:31).

Paul and Silas prayed and sang songs in the inner cell of a Philippian jail at midnight. The strength of their prayer shook the jail itself. It even resulted in the salvation of the jailer.

Prayer is invincible--impossible to subdue.

The act of praying generates omnipotence. Prayer gives the frail human reed unshakable strength.

Prayer is like radium--a source of luminous self-generating energy.

All that prayer can do never has been defined. It is still a great world for research and exploitation.

Pray without ceasing and you will know dominion in prayer! Continual communion with the Commander assures victory.

6. SINGING. One of the most dramatic and powerful demonstrations of dominion is singing.

The entire nation of Israel sang as they crossed the Red Sea. *"The Lord is my strength and song. . ."* were some of the words in their song of triumph (Exodus 15).

Deborah and Barak sang a song of victory (Judges 5).

Paul and Silas sang in the Philippian jail. Their shackles fell off and the gates flung open.

Singing brings release to the spirit.

Almost all nations have national anthems which raise the spirit of their people. All marching armies sing militant songs as they march into war.

New Testament believers are told to *"be filled with the Spirit; Speaking to yourselves in psalms and hymns and spiritual songs, singing and making melody in your heart to the Lord"* (Ephesians 5:18,19).

God's people should sing the song of victory which gives added strength as an emblem of dominion.

7. ACTION. God does not give power to the inactive.

Jesus said, *"He that believeth on me, the works*

that I do shall he DO. . . ." (John 14:12).

Dominion means TO DO. Dominion is an ACT and not an idea.

Throughout history, those who possessed dominion were men and women of action for God.

God told Moses to tell the children of Israel to step into the water. He told Moses to stretch forth his rod. God did the rest. The waters of the Red Sea rolled back and made a path.

Jesus told a man with a withered hand, *"Stretch it forth."* Jesus did the rest. The man's hand was restored whole as his other hand.

In most instances in God's Word, action was necessary before dominion was realized. The children of Israel had to march around Jericho's walls before they fell. Naaman had to dip seven times in Jordan before his leprosy was cleansed.

Works alone are not sufficient for salvation or dominion. But some action is necessary--even vital.

Paul reminded the Corinthian Christians that there is work to do for the kingdom of God. *"For we are labourers together with God"* (1 Corinthians 3:9).

In the second chapter of James, even stronger language is employed. *"What doth it profit, my brethren, though a man say he hath faith, and have not works? can faith save him?. . .Even so faith, if it hath not works, is dead, being alone"* (vv. 14,17).

The word translated "works" here implies action. One translation reads, *"Faith without corresponding actions is dead."*

It is not enough to know God's will--you must DO IT. *"Not with eyeservice, as menpleasers; but as the servants of Christ, DOING THE WILL OF GOD from the heart"* (Ephesians 6:6).

One could know he had money in the bank and still go hungry and cold. He must go to the bank, withdraw some cash from his account, and spend it for food and warm clothing before his needs can be met.

Having it is not enough. Knowing he has it is not enough. There must be action--the money must be used before it is of any value in meeting his needs.

So it is with Christian dominion. Before it pays off with bountiful blessings, dominion must be put in force with action on the part of the believer.

In reality, dominion is an instrument to better enable the disciple to work for God and to obey His commandments.

His commandments have always been: Go. . . Do. . . Give. . . Work. . .

By *using* the pertinent instruments of dominion, any believer can be a triumphant Christian. Therefore, I urge you to stand up and have dominion with Christ. Be an overcomer and a blesser of mankind all the days of your life.

God Gave Me Dominion

God gave me dominion in my spirit--this happened the day of my new birth. Therefore, I can exert dominion in my soul--in my mind, my emotions, and my will. I can exert dominion in my body.

In my total person I experience dominion every day.

God told me to "Look like dominion. Walk like dominion. Talk like dominion."

I am to act like dominion.

You see, the day I discovered Christ as my Savior, I literally discovered Dominion!

Chapter 7

HISTORY'S
PEOPLE OF DOMINION

The annals of man's story are alive with the beautiful history of people who exercised dominion on this earth.

To read the eleventh chapter of Hebrews is to read an account of amazing use of dominion.

It begins with Abel (v. 4). God records that Abel walked in power so great *"he, being dead, yet speaketh."* He could not be silenced! Until this moment he guides men's thinking in how to give to God. For the Lord said that he made an *"excellent sacrifice."*

Enoch is unparalleled (v. 5). He was a man of unique dominion. At a time when it was not popular to walk with God, he walked with God. When others found it difficult to find God, he not only found Him but he walked with Him. He communed with Him. While every other person of his generation died and had a funeral ceremony, he was divinely translated to heaven and left behind a testimony that he had pleased God.

Noah knew dominion (v. 7). He preached a sermon no one else preached. And his generation would not believe it. He stood completely alone. He accepted an arduous task and became a deliverer of the human race. He broke the bondage of the antediluvians and brought the human race under the scintillating power of the rainbow to live under the promise it was a sign of forever.

One could find no greater man of dominion than Abraham (vv. 8-10). He had the courage to leave his home, country, and people. He had courage to go into the unknown. He had courage to wage wars against superior numbers. He defeated four kings and their armies with his house servants of three hundred and eighteen men (Genesis 14).

Abraham knew and lived dominion in every area. He communicated with God. He was very rich--and he knew how to handle his riches (Genesis 13). He believed God to become the father of God's chosen people.

Moses had to be a man of dominion (vv. 23-27). He led that murmuring multitude of millions, which Abraham's family had become, out of Egypt's bondage, through the wilderness, and to the Promised Land. He so possessed his own soul that at the height of their rebellion he pleaded for them before God, *"Yet now, if thou wilt forgive their sin--; and if not, blot me, I pray thee, out of thy book"* (Exodus 32:32).

Moses was a man of choice. Hebrews says that *"he*

refused" to be called the son of Pharaoh's daughter. *"He chose"* to suffer affliction with the people of God, rather than to enjoy the pleasures of sin for a season. *"He esteemed"* the reproach of Christ greater riches than the treasures in Egypt. *"He forsook"* Egypt. *"He did not fear"* the wrath of the king. He held the reins in the face of Satan and delivered God's people from his hands.

The harlot Rahab was born outside the nation of Israel and its promises (v. 31). It would seem that her fate was sealed. But though her entire city perished --she perished not. She had the courage to believe something not one of her people believed. She believed that the God of Israel was *"God in heaven above, and in earth below"* (Joshua 2:11). For she had heard that forty years before He had dried up the Red Sea for them and had defeated their enemies (Joshua 2:10). Others had surely heard it, too. But Rahab believed and acted. She took control of the reins of her life and saved herself and her family.

This chapter in Hebrews lists others too numerous to write about such as Joshua, Gideon, Samson, David, Samuel, the prophets, and many others.

Then in the next chapter God says in a tremendous revelation, *"Wherefore seeing we also are compassed about with so great a cloud of witnesses, let us lay aside every weight, and the sin which doth so easily beset us, and let us run with patience the race that is set before us"* (Hebrews 12:1).

A New People of Dominion

It has been my joy to know people of strength who refused to be dominated by fears or circumstances, running the race well that was set before them.

My mother, Betty Sumrall, was a person of dominion. I observed her life some fifty years. When the odds were great against her, she knew she would win. She was sure of the Word of God and was sure that God was performing His promises. She lived a victorious life of dominion.

For a number of years I was closely associated with Howard Carter of London, England. He was a man who knew dominion in its deepest manifestation. The British government could not break it down when it placed him in prison during World War I for being a conscientious objector. In a cramped prison cell, God gave him a revelation of the gifts of the Spirit and their operation in the Church that is recognized around the world today. Until the end of his days he lived victoriously with dominion.

One of the strongest men of dominion I have had contact with was Smith Wigglesworth of Bradford, England. I first met him at a national conference in Wales. He was the teacher in the afternoon service and I was the evangelist in the evening. He invited me to his home. Thereafter I visited him on a number of occasions.

Smith Wigglesworth dominated any scene where

he was placed. In Australia he was in a very large restaurant. He noticed that scarcely anyone bowed their heads to pray over their food.

When his food was served, he clinked the side of his glass with his knife, stood up, and said so that all could hear, "Ladies and gentlemen--I have observed that almost none of you prayed over your food. You can now lay down your knife and fork and I will pray over it for you."

With this he prayed a strong prayer. Then he said, "Thank you. Let us all eat."

He got a number of congratulations and two people were converted in that restaurant.

Wherever he went, dominion was a part of him.

He told me personally that when he awoke in the morning, he never asked Smith Wigglesworth how he felt. But the first ten minutes of his day were used to praise and magnify God, thanking God for his salvation, and for the way he would be blessed that day.

Few men in our generation have known the strength and dominion God placed in his heart.

Reverend Howard Carter and I conducted a special conference in Stockholm, Sweden for Pastor Lewi Pethrus. I felt a very close relationship with Pastor Pethrus. I observed in him spiritual strength. He had known many difficulties, he had faced many problems, but he was a winner. His great church--at that time the largest full gospel church in the world-- was part of his remarkable life of dominion in Christ.

It certainly was exciting to know such people.

And I believe there are multitudes, as of this moment, who know dominion because of Jesus' power, and who will go down in history as people of dominion.

I have just learned of one such man. He is a pastor in the underground church in the Soviet Union. His story was told to me by someone who knows him personally and who just visited in his home.

In the midst of darkness, I was told, this man looks like, walks like, and talks like dominion. Several times he had opportunity to leave the country, but he chose to stay because he believed God wanted him to remain. So he and his wife and children stayed.

He has been imprisoned a total of thirteen years. He spent several of those years in Siberia.

During one term, prison officials desired to make an example of him. They paraded the small man with the shining face before the entire prison populace saying, "This is the worst criminal in this prison."

Later, on work details, other prisoners began to make their way to him. "What terrible crime did you commit?" they wanted to know.

"I steal," he answered.

"What do you steal?"

"I steal souls from the devil!"

Whereupon he proceeded to commit the very crime upon the inquiring soul.

Dominion certainly is available to each one of us. The decision is ours. Let's decide to be victorious in Jesus!

Chapter 8

PEOPLE WHO REFUSE TO EXERCISE DOMINION

History actually reverberates with men and women who, because of fear, did not exercise dominion. The Bible also gives us the end of such people.

Listed here are seven areas where the devil would like to attack your dominion through fear.

1. FEAR OF CHANGE. Many people could have been prosperous if they were not fearful of change. Actually, what makes a person old is that he refuses change. In our vernacular, we say he is "set in his ways." This literally means he refuses to change. Fear of a change in jobs, or location to live, or of changing friends often destroys the powers of dominion.

2. FEAR OF PEOPLE. It is the devil's trick to make us afraid of people. In the Book of Nehemiah, his enemies tried to get Nehemiah to be afraid. Nehemiah responded to their hired prophet, *"Should such a man as I flee (or run and hide)?"* Nehemiah knew dominion and had no fear.

71

Sometimes people fear the boss. He is overbearing; he curses. Sometimes people fear to witness of their relationship with Jesus.

God told His prophet Jeremiah not to fear their faces. We must never fear people.

3. FEAR OF THE UNKNOWN. A person can never have dominion if he has fear of the unknown. God commands the unknown. A positive force and power is stronger than a negative force or power. We know God has His hand on tomorrow and we are not afraid of the unknown.

4. FEAR OF RESPONSIBILITIES. No person can enjoy dominion if he fears to take on greater responsibilities. Those who are willing to stay at the bottom because they cannot accept responsibility will never know the joys of dominion.

5. FEAR OF FAILURE. Possibly there is nothing so destroying of the powers of dominion as the stalking fear of failure. It is the devil who fosters such a fear. The Spirit of Jesus does not know failure. When we are linked with Him, it is impossible to fail. Fear of failure is of the devil and must be destroyed before one can enjoy the delicious fruits of dominion.

6. FEAR OF ADDED WORK. You would be amazed at the millions of people who are fearful of what added work would do to them. They do not realize that while they are worrying about it, they could accomplish it. Additional work is spiritual growth and material growth. The devil's fears are always fanciful and erroneous. We must never fear taking on added jobs.

7. *FEAR OF PHYSICAL OR MENTAL BREAK-DOWN.* Too many men and woman are tormented by fear of breakdown--that is, the disintegration of their strength and moral courage. Job said that what he greatly feared came upon him.

We must rebuke all such fear and be part of that select group who have dominion and are not listed with those who refuse to exercise it. Remember:

> *For God hath not given us the spirit of*
> *fear; but of power, and of love, and of a*
> *sound mind.*
>
> -- 2 Timothy 1:7

Rebuke the devil and he will flee from you. Rebuke fear and it will flee from you.

Men as Grasshoppers

In Numbers, chapter thirteen, we see twelve select leaders of Israel were sent into Palestine to spy out the Land of Promise. Ten of them returned with what the Bible calls an *"evil report."*

They said, in effect, *"The land is good. The country is beautiful. It is rich and desirable, BUT GIANTS LIVE THERE."* They told Moses, *"We are AS GRASSHOPPERS before them."*

The nation of Israel accepted their evil report. They already had forgotten how God brought them out of Egypt--not through their strength, but in His power. They already had forgotten the miracles that took place in the desert. And now, by refusing the dominion that belonged to them, they turned and went into the Sinai desert, where for forty years they wandered round and round in a waterless land until they all died. Not one of the adults who accepted that report of fear entered the Promised Land.

God had said, "The land is yours."

The devil had said, "You are too small, too weak, and too insignificant."

They obeyed the wrong source of information.

Judas and Dominion

Acts 1:25 says that by transgression Judas failed. It was not an accident. It was no weakness on God's part. It was not because there was not sufficient power. It was because he refused dominion. He yielded himself to the devil--and in so doing he lost his life.

We all know people who have refused to exercise divine dominion. Some die premature deaths. Some fail in business. Some permit the devil to destroy their homes, when if they would accept the Scriptures, they would know glorious victory.

Our trust must always be in Jesus. He gives us the dominion and He can sustain us in every moment of adversity.

74

Chapter 9

COLLECTIVE DOMINION

Satan not only will steal personal dominion, rulership, and authority, causing an individual to be a slave--but the devil works very hard to enslave entire communities, cities, and nations.

He can do this through a lying philosophy taught in schools or churches. Empires are destroyed through lies which lead to weakness.

Pagan religions enslave entire nations. From the highest to the lowest the people bow down in fear before superstitions and lies. They obey that which they know not. These nations abound in fear, poverty, disease, and all that Satan brought with him into the earth.

BUT GOD OFFERS COLLECTIVE DOMINION TO THOSE WHO WILL ACCEPT IT!

Communities of Dominion

Abraham's pilgrims became a large community.

He had 318 armed servants. They defeated and destroyed four kings and their armies. The battle became the first recorded conflict in the Bible.

How exciting it must have been to have lived in that community. General Abraham, himself, trained and equipped the army. He taught his men they could conquer at great odds because of added power --Jehovah God's power! It worked!

Cities of Dominion

There are cities in the world where the saints of God have taken dominion over entire areas.

This was true in Zion, Illinois for many years. It was founded as a Christian city. For a long period of time no cigarettes or alcoholic beverages were permitted in any form. People could sense the Spirit of the Lord as they entered the area.

So-called "evangelical cities" have a very different "feeling" than pagan cities. For example, I found Calcutta, India, with its millions of Hindu gods, to be one of the most depressing cities on the face of the earth. The city is named after a female goddess named Cali. Cali is a fierce devil. When you see her image at the great temple, her tongue sticks out about six inches wide and eight inches long. This goddess demands blood. Her followers bring goats to the temple and cut their throats, letting the blood flow into a groove under the hideous idol. Her devotees splash their faces and drink the hot goat blood. I have been there several times. It is sickening. The entire area reeks of Satan. Sin, sickness, poverty, and death reign. Anyone can see it. Anyone can "feel" it.

On the other hand, there are several cities in the United States today which are especially possessed by God's people and His Spirit. Many great works of the kingdom of God usually go forth from them. When you enter the city, the very atmosphere about you warms your total being.

Someone I know lives in a small town near such a city. (The entire area is affected by the dominion of the saints in that city.) The pastor of a small church walked by the corner bar one morning on his way to the post office. He had been going by that bar for years. But that morning he placed his hand on the old brick wall and cursed the bar in the same manner that his Master had gone by a fig tree and cursed it one morning two thousand years before.

In a few weeks, the bar closed. Someone reopened it. It closed again. The pastor almost had forgotten what he had done when the Spirit of the Lord reminded him.

The young woman who was youth director of the church was impressed by the Spirit of God to possess the bar. After much hard work, the former bar reopened to youth work and street meetings.

A few doors down the street was the ancient pool hall. The young youth workers decided to possess that. Within a few more months the pool hall went out of business and a "re-creation center" to reach the restless young people Satan was out to wreck was opened.

This small town is being possessed by the people of God who will take their dominion.

It is interesting to me that Jesus wept over Jerusalem. It was the big city of His life.

Today, we should weep over the great cities of our land lest they become throne rooms of the devil's power.

There is no power which can stand before the living church. The Lord Jesus promised that even the gates of hell could not stop His Church. Let's advance on the big cities. Let's possess our communities for Christ.

New Jerusalem: The City of God

Abraham looked for a city which has foundations, whose builder and maker is God (Hebrews 11:10). And so do we.

The prophet Ezekiel described it in glorious detail.

The New Testament makes our hearts yearn for its conditions of sublime dominion.

> *But ye are come unto mount Sion, and unto the city of the living God, the heavenly Jerusalem. . . .*
> -- Hebrews 12:22

> *Him that overcometh will I make a pillar in the temple of my God, and he shall go no*

*more out: and I will write upon him the
name of my God, and the name of the city
of my God, which is new Jerusalem, which
cometh down out of heaven from my
God. . . .*

-- Revelation 3:12

*And I saw a new heaven and a new
earth: for the first heaven and the first
earth were passed away; and there was no
more sea.*

*And I John saw the holy city, new
Jerusalem, coming down from God out of
heaven, prepared as a bride adorned for her
husband.*

*And I heard a great voice out of heaven
saying, Behold, the tabernacle of God is
with me, and he will dwell with them,
and they shall be his people, and God himself shall be with them, and be their God.*

*And God shall wipe away all tears from
their eyes; and there shall be no more
death, neither sorrow, nor crying, neither
shall there be any more pain: for the former things are passed away.*

-- Revelation 21:1-4

Here God's Word paints a picture of a city where
divine dominion reigns supreme. The things that are
absent are the things Satan brought with him when he
usurped man's rule.

> *And he carried me away in the spirit*
> *to a great and high mountain, and shewed*
> *me that great city, the holy Jerusalem,*
> *descending out of heaven from God, Hav-*
> *ing the glory of God. . .*
>
> *And I saw no temple therein: for the*
> *Lord God Almighty and the Lamb are the*
> *temple of it.*
>
> *And the city had no need of the sun,*
> *neither of the moon, to shine in it: for the*
> *glory of God did lighten it, and the Lamb*
> *is the light thereof.*
>
> -- Revelation 21:10,11,22,23

God's glory fills the city.

Every citizen is a victor. Every person a redeemed and immortal one.

But God's glory fills His temple in the earth today. We, the Church, are that living temple. When we take the dominion that is now ours, His glory will effectually lighten the places we possess. For the Lamb is our light indeed.

Nations of Dominion

When Israel honored God no enemy could stand before her. If they came before her one way, they fled before her seven ways. The Red Sea's waters rolled back to let her through. Jericho's walls tumbled before her. Canaan's inhabitants were no match for her God. The All-Sufficient One was her Provider. The Lord of Hosts was her Healer. The Most High God was her Strength and Shield. It was His desire that everyone should look at her obvious dominion over all the power of the enemy and say, "There is a God in Israel!" Then, like Rahab, they would want to know Him as their God.

But nations, like individuals, must serve God by choice. God set before Israel her choices.

> *I call heaven and earth to record this day against you, that I have set before you life and death, blessing and cursing: therefore choose life, that both thou and thy seed may live:*
>
> *That thou mayest love the Lord thy God, and that thou mayest obey his voice, and that thou mayest cleave unto him: for he is thy life, and the length of thy days: that thou mayest dwell in the land which the Lord sware unto thy fathers, to Abraham, to Isaac, and to Jacob, to give them.*
> -- Deuteronomy 30:19,20

Ancient Israel forsook her God to worship devils (Deuteronomy 32:17). When she did, she gave up her dominion. Her inhabitants were dispersed throughout the earth. Her land lay idle and desolate for hundreds of years.

The United States of America is one of the most

unique nations of all times. Early settlers came to her shores seeking religious freedom. In-depth studies into Virginia's earliest visitors from Europe reveal startling facts of the leading of the Spirit of God.

Through our years we have been known to the world as a Christian nation. "In God We Trust" is stamped upon our money. "One nation, under God," is recited in our pledge of allegiance to our flag.

Even today the Gospel goes forth from this nation as no other in history. The huge majority of all missionary work is supported from this nation by the sacrificial giving of its blessed Christians.

Freedom to worship. Freedom to assemble. Freedom of speech. Freedom of the press. All these are birthrights often unappreciated by the blessed ones born within the USA's domain.

She has blessed Israel and known the blessing which results according to God's Word (Genesis 12:3).

But in our lifetime, we have seen our nation lose for the first time in her history.

In 1956, America took a position against Israel. She demanded that France and Britain remove their troops from the Suez Canal Zone. She demanded Israel to give back to Egypt the entire Sinai which Israel had taken in battle. America cut off relations with Israel. Not a plane was permitted to land and no ship could dock. My family and I lived in Jerusalem at that time. It was France that fed us.

From that time, America has lost ground and glory in Korea, Vietnam, Cuba, Africa, Asia, So. America.

Nations can be hurt.

But nations can be helped. God has placed the state of a nation into the hands of His people who dwell there.

> *If my people, which are called by my name, shall humble themselves, and pray, and seek my face, and turn from their wicked ways; then will I hear from heaven, and will forgive their sin, and will heal their land.*
> -- 2 Chronicles 7:14

God's people in a land can exercise their collective dominion. They can hold the reins of the land in their hands.

Christians everywhere should practice the following New Testament admonition to pray for the leaders of their government--first of all.

> *I exhort therefore, that, first of all, supplications, prayers, intercessions, and giving of thanks, be made for all men;*
> *For kings, and for all that are in authority; that we may lead a quiet and peaceable life in all godliness and honesty.*
> *For this is good and acceptable in the sight of God our Saviour;*
> *Who will have all men to be saved, and to come unto the knowledge of the truth.*
> -- 1 Timothy 2:1-4

The Church in the United States is responsible before God for this nation. Let us rise up and take our dominion on behalf of our nation--and on the behalf of the countless millions of lost humanity whom "God would have to be saved, and to come unto the knowledge of the truth" through the Gospel that must continue to go forth freely from the United States of America.

Chapter 10

SEVEN STEPS TO DOMINION

God's Word is the only source for you to learn how you personally can have dominion.

First, the Scriptures reveal the arena of conflict. Let's examine this vital revelation in three translations:

> *For we wrestle not against flesh and blood, but against principalities, against powers, against the rulers of the darkness of this world, against spiritual wickedness in high places.*
>
> -- Ephesians 6:12 King James Version

> *For ours is not a conflict with mere flesh and blood, but with the despotisms, the empires, the forces that control and govern this dark world--the spiritual hosts of evil arrayed against us in the heavenly warfare.*
>
> -- Ephesians 6:12 Weymouth

We have to struggle, not with flesh and blood, but with the angelic rulers, the angelic authorities, the potentates of the dark present, the spirit-forces of evil in the heavenly sphere; so take God's armour; praying with all manner of prayer.

-- Ephesians 6:12,18 Moffatt

The Holy Spirit, through the Apostle Paul, told us that our battle is not with *"flesh and blood."* Our battle is not with humans. Our battle is not with denominations or organizations. Our battle is spiritual.

Seven Steps

Study these seven steps--gleaned from God's Word --for genuine progress toward dominion in your personal life.

1. *RECOGNIZE YOUR SOURCE OF DOMINION.* In Ephesians 1:17-23, Paul prayed a prayer for Christians. He specifically requested that God grant them *"the spirit of wisdom and revelation"* concerning certain vital truths. He knew they needed to understand some things. One thing he wanted them to know was:

. . .what is the exceeding greatness of his power to usward who believe. . . .

-- Ephesians 1:19

You and I must understand the exceeding greatness of His power directed toward us who believe. We must know the exceeding greatness of God's power flowing through us.

Paul's Holy Spirit given prayer describes this mighty strength directed toward us as:

> . . .*according to the working of his mighty power,*
>
> *which he wrought in Christ, when he raised him from the dead, and set him at his own right hand in the heavenly places,*
>
> *Far above all principality, and power, and might, and dominion, and every name that is named, not only in this world, but also in that which is to come:*
>
> *And hath put all things under his feet, and gave him to be the head over all things to the church,*
>
> *Which is his body, the fulness of him that filleth all in all.*
>
> -- Ephesians 1:19-23

Recognize your source of power!

Our power comes directly from headquarters--and headquarters is in Heaven.

We have a daily source of strength and power the world knows nothing about. The world cannot tap in on it. The only way to get into this power is to get into Jesus. The only way to get into Jesus is to believe on Him. The only way to believe on Him is to accept Him as your Lord and Savior (Romans 10:9,10). When Jesus becomes Lord of your life, this exceedingly great power is yours.

Recognize your source. And recognize what is not your source. Your source is not human mind. Your source is not human strength. <u>Your source is God!</u>

2. *LEARN THE EFFECTIVE USE OF THE WEAPONS OF DOMINION.* Just as the conflict is spiritual--so are the weapons.

> *For though we walk in the flesh, we do not war after the flesh:*
> *(For the weapons of our warfare are not carnal, but mighty through God to the pulling down of strong holds.)*
> -- 2 Corinthians 10:3,4

Learn to use these God-given instruments of our warfare:

THE WORD OF GOD. Every victorious Christian must learn how to effectively use the Bible, the Word of God. The Bible is our sword (Ephesians 6:17). People of dominion must effectively use the sword God has given us. Revelation 1:16 pictures Jesus with a sharp two-edged sword coming out of His mouth. With God's Word in your heart and in your mouth you will dominate Satan in every instance as surely as Jesus did in the wilderness. It is written!

The Bible is the source of spiritual food that we

might eat and be strong (1 Peter 2:2). Christians who feed their spirits daily on the Word of God will grow spiritually. Their spirits, strong and well-nourished, will dominate their beings. Rather than being ruled by the outward man, the inner man will rule over their mind, will, emotions, and flesh. Stalwart and strong, they will know their God and do exploits in His name.

PRAYER. If you do not know prayer, you do not know the power of God. Prayer is the most talked about, discussed, and the least used power available to mankind.

Oil, undiscovered, is an untapped resource. Coal, not mined, is an untapped source of power. But the greatest source of untapped power and resource is prayer.

Through personal communication with the Creator, people can do things they could never before do.

In his article, "Man the Unknown" published in Reader's Digest, Dr. Alexis Carrel said: "As a physician, I have seen men, after all other therapy had failed, lifted out of disease and melancholy by the serene effort of prayer. It is the only power in the world that seems to overcome the so-called 'laws of nature'. . . ."

It is in prayer that decisions are made. It is in prayer that God directs us. It is in prayer that God does great things in our lives. Lord, teach us to pray!

FAITH. Poetically, faith has been called the eye that sees the invisible, the ear that hears the inaudible, the hand that feels the intangible, and the power that works the impossible.

Jesus said, *"All things are possible to him that believeth"* (Mark 9:23).

Faith is a weapon. Faith speaks (Mark 11:23). Faith is the voice of authority. One can speak words of faith to bring forth things which never would be brought forth otherwise.

Faith is an act. Martin Luther gave this view of faith: "It is a busy, active, living reality that does not ask, 'What shall I do?' but before it has time to ask, it is up and doing." David believed Goliath would be defeated, so he hurled a stone at his head. Faith acts.

Faith is a way of life--a walk with God. The great miracles which characterized Smith Wigglesworth's ministry, I believe, were the result of his close walk with God. He talked with God so often and for so long, God's ear was very near to him. And when he made a request of God it was easy for God to understand. The tendency of many is to walk so far from God that it is not possible to hear Him when He speaks. But the person of dominion will walk with God. He will not seek faith--he will live faith. Living faith, the life of God, will flow from his innermost being.

How do you get faith? The rule is simply this:

> *Faith cometh by hearing, and hearing by the word of God.*
> -- Romans 10:17

The Word alone is the source of faith. But the Word will not build faith unless it becomes a part of your very being. Jesus said, *"If ye abide in me, and my words abide in you, ye shall ask what ye will, and it shall be done unto you"* (John 15:7).

WITNESSING. Witnessing is a weapon. When you witness to someone, you get something back. He that blesses is blessed. He that gives is given unto. He that watereth is watered. As we reach out to bless and love others, God reaches back and replenishes us, giving us of His divine blessings. Witnessing to others about the power of God in your life will cause you to stand up stronger, and stronger, and stronger.

3. RECOGNIZE YOUR RELATIONSHIP TO THE BODY OF BELIEVERS--AND THE BODY'S DIVINE RELATIONSHIP WITH CHRIST. The most powerful living organism on the earth today is the Church--the very Body of Christ. Jesus Christ is the Head of this Body. Every born-again believer is a member of His powerful Body.

> *And he is the head of the body, the church: who is the beginning, the firstborn from the dead; that in all things he might have the preeminence.*
> -- Colossians 1:18

> *Now ye are the body of Christ, and members in particular.*
> -- 1 Corinthians 12:27

91

Jesus Himself described this Body's irresistible strength. .

> *. . .I will build my church; and the gates of hell shall not prevail against it.*
>
> -- Matthew 16:18

For many centuries the Church too little recognized her indomitable power. But you and I are living in a day when this powerful organism is waking up-- ready to arise and shine as the prophet Isaiah foretold (Isaiah 60).

We must get the revelation that we are the Body of Christ. We must accept the spiritual authority we have in the Body of Christ. We must accept the fact that the gates of hell cannot prevail against us. As we move together, nothing can stand before us. We can change anything we want to change on the face of this earth.

Jesus said it. I didn't say it. Jesus declared that the gates of hell cannot prevail against the Church, the Living Body of Christ.

It will strengthen you personally to recognize your relationship to the Church. And for personal victory, be closely related to Christ's Body of believers. I do not believe you can annul the Body of Christ and be strong in the Lord. Our relationship one with another is very important.

Some say, "It doesn't mean anything if I don't go to church." That is the devil talking through their lips.

We minister to each other. People sitting in the pews have set me on fire as I preached. Something in me rose up as I looked at them. If they had stayed home, I wouldn't have gotten that inspiration, that blessing. I've been so blessed shaking someone's hand that I didn't want to let go.

People who stay home are selfish. You can never be good in God and be selfish.

> *Even when we were dead in sins, hath quickened us together with Christ (by grace ye are saved;)*
> *And hath raised us up together, and made us sit together in heavenly places in Christ Jesus.*
>
> -- Ephesians 2:5,6

We are to sit together in spiritual places in Christ Jesus.

> *Not forsaking the assembling of ourselves together, as the manner of some is; but exhorting one another: and so much the more, as ye see the day approaching.*
>
> -- Hebrews 10:25

We see the day approaching!

A good friend of mine held a responsible position with a large firm. His company asked him to transfer to another area of the country. They offered him a far better wage.

This man traveled to the area and searched for a church he liked. When he could not find one, he returned and said to his boss, "I don't want the new position."

His superior said, "Why don't you want the job? Isn't it good?"

He said, "I suppose it is. But I can't find a church I want to worship in there. So I don't want the job."

His boss could not understand. He refused the advancement because he couldn't find the kind of church he wanted in which to worship, learn, grow, fellowship, and work.

Tens of thousands have backslidden because of moving into places where there was not a good place to worship. Almost every day I hear someone say, "I can't find a good church where I live." I say, "Why did you move there?"

The most important thing in life is your spirit, soul, and body--not your pocketbook. The most important thing in the world is for your children to have a good place--a precious place to worship God.

Recognize your relationship with the living Body of Christ. That is the path of victory and dominion.

4. IDENTIFY YOUR ENEMY. If you don't know who your enemy is, you won't be able to win a victory. You won't know where to deliver a blow.

If you think your enemy is your wife, or your husband, or your children, or the church, you will never be able to win a victory. And striking out at the wrong foe only makes matters worse.

First identify your enemy. Satan is the enemy of God and the enemy of God's creation, mankind. When Satan strikes at the human personality, it is imperative to recognize the source of the trouble.

Rather than getting grouchy and grumpy, get into a state of prayer and say, "Let me see here. My wife is a sweet person, so it is not her. This is from the devil. I am going to resist him." Close your hand and say, "Satan, in the name of Jesus Christ of Nazareth, I command you to take your hand off my business. Get your hand off my house. And get out of here NOW!"

You will have identified your enemy. You will have successfully stopped his tactics. And you won't be fighting your family.

5. *KNOW THE WEAKNESS OF YOUR ENEMY.* The devil is completely defeated by the Lord Jesus Christ. He can't do anything against Jesus. No devil or demon anywhere can combat the Holy Spirit. The apostles of the Lord brought great fear in the hearts of demons--they cried out and ran away from the disciples' presence. And any true believer can resist the devil today--he still has to flee when Christians resist him.

> *Submit yourselves therefore to God. Resist the devil, and he will flee from you.*
> -- James 4:7

We do not necessarily have to fight the devil. We

have to remind him of Calvary where the Lord Jesus Christ defeated him. Remind him of his complete defeat. Remind him of his ultimate destiny--hell. Tell him, "Don't you know what is ahead of you? Don't you know where you are going to endure eternity?" Then tell him that you know he is a defeated foe.

Satan is limited. He is limited by his fallen estate. (At one time he was an archangel.) He is limited by Christ's resurrection which cut him short and stripped from him the keys of hell and of death (Rev. 1:18).

Satan has a bruised head which cannot be healed. God foretold it in the Garden of Eden. He said the Seed of the woman was coming (Genesis 3:15). This Child of a virgin would bruise Satan's head--He would break Satan's lordship. The devil and all his cohorts remember Jesus Christ fulfilling this prophecy and bringing them *"to nought"* (1 Corinthians 2:6-8).

All evil spirits--brought to nothing by the Lord of Glory--fear and tremble before a person who has the power and the anointing and the authority of God.

Do not talk about how big and strong the devil is. If you do, you will believe it. But remind him that he has already lost the mighty warfare. Remind him he is under your feet and you are walking on top of him (Ephesians 1:19-23). He understands that.

6. STAY READY FOR BATTLE AT ALL TIMES. We have an enemy whose key strategy is to keep the Christian away from his place of authority and spiritual power -- "off base" so to speak.

Be aware of his tactics. Immediately resist and

throw off from yourself any of the following states Satan may try to put upon you:

VEXATION. If Satan can keep you vexed, you cannot cast out devils. If he can keep you angry with someone, you cannot heal the sick.

DEPRESSION. If the devil can get you depressed, you are not effective in the Kingdom. You cannot go around in sadness and give people gladness. Sadness and gladness don't come out of the same jug.

Depression can come from many sources. It can come from sources in the home, sources at work, sources in the body. Events can take place.

Depression can even get to you from listening to the news. If it does, turn off the news and read two or three chapters in the Bible. News reports don't give a clear picture of things anyway. Most give their ideas about things, and their ideas sometimes have to do with perverted minds.

CONFUSION. Life is simple. You only have to make one decision at a time. And if you make it under God, don't keep making it all day long. Don't take the dress back to the store forty times. Keep it when you buy it.

If the devil can get you confused, you will not be effective.

Stop for a moment and say, "My name is Sam Jones. My address is so-and-so. I work at such-and-such a place. I am married to Mary Jones and I have so-many children. I am saved and filled with the Holy Spirit. I belong to such-and-such church. Devil, I don't need to know much else, so get out of my way."

The devil does not want you to be ready for battle. He wants you in a state of confusion. If you are, you are not ready for battle.

But you don't have to live in a state of confusion! The devil is a liar. There is victory in Jesus!

Anything that is not clear today will be clear tomorrow. Just rejoice in everything today and God will make the thing clear for you.

SELFISHNESS. If the devil can get you to be self-centered, to keep looking at yourself, and to be selfish in your innermost being, you will not be ready. You will be constantly wondering, "How am I getting along? What can I do for myself? Me. . .My. . .Me. . . My. . ."

Be Christ-centered. Say, "Lord, I am out to win souls, and I don't mean maybe! Devil, we're coming after them. They belong to Jesus, and you can't have them!"

The devil would like Christians to be so self-centered about their businesses and homes that they lose the vision of the world.

I was in China when a Chinese communist told me this, "You have more missionaries than we have communists in China--but we are going to take China. Do you know why?"

I said, "Why?"

He said, "You teach people to give ten percent. We teach them to give one hundred percent. I give everything to the party. We are going to win."

I just stared at him. I hardly knew what to say, but I can assure you that as long as you are self-centered you are not dynamite. Lose self-centeredness and get lost in the great love of God. Love the world. Love the people of your community. Then you are ready to defeat the devil.

7. *REJOICE IN VICTORY.* Jesus said, *"Whatsoever ye shall bind on earth shall be bound in heaven: and whatsoever ye shall loose on earth shall be loosed in heaven. . .For where two or three are gathered together in my name, there am I in the midst of them"* (Matthew 18:18-20).

The devil is subject to the believer's faith; he can't do anything about it.

The devil is subject to the believer's authority; he can't do anything about it.

The devil is subject to the believer's rights; he can't do anything about them.

The devil is subject to the words a believer speaks, and he can't do anything about it.

The devil resists, but if the believer cries out to him to go, he must go!

Therefore believers must lift up their voices and praise God for it. We must rejoice in victory at all times.

We are not losers--we are all winners! Jesus is coming soon and we will be ready to meet Him in the air.

Whatever happens to the Arab oil is one thing--I know what is going to happen to the oil of the Holy

Spirit. I am receiving more of it all the time. I keep pouring it in and pouring it in--and the supply is not short. The price has not gone up a bit in two thousand years. Just be certain you have the right kind of oil.

God wants us to be glad in victory. God wants us to go throughout the city saying, "Jesus already has won! The Church already is victorious!"

If the devil says something about it, stop him by saying, "Shut up, in Jesus' name. I am just informing you that we already have won the battle."

There is victory in Jesus. Whatever you need, He already has won for you. Just claim what is yours in His name.

If you are sick say, "I thank You, Father, that Jesus has obtained my healing. I receive it now in His name. Thank You. I have it now."

Remember! *You are what God says you are! You can do what God says you can do!*

Chapter 11

LIMITS OF HUMAN DOMINION

God created man for dominion. And only God can set the boundaries of human dominion. He read out the limitations and expansions of mankind's dominion in the beginning:

> *. . . let them have dominion over the fish of the sea, and over the fowl of the air, and over the cattle, and over all the earth, and over every creeping thing that creepeth upon the earth.*
>
> -- Genesis 1:26

> *Thou madest him (man) to have dominion over the works of thy hands: thou hast put all things under his feet.*
>
> -- Psalm 8:6

Only Christ Himself is master of all dominion in

heaven and earth. Consummating His colossal achievement of world redemption, the resurrected Christ
proclaimed, *"All power is given unto me in heaven
and in earth"* (Matthew 28:18).

What unlimited, unrivaled, and incalculable dominion and strength are involved in that universal proclamation.

Christ is unlimited!

His power--omnipotent!

His presence--omnipresent!

But the wonder of it all is the command He gave
His followers immediately upon the heels of His "All-
Power" proclamation. Notice that it came with al-
most the same breath:

> *All power is given unto me in heaven and
> in earth. GO YE THEREFORE. . . .*
> -- Matthew 28:18,19

Only Christ Himself can set the boundaries or cate-
gories of dominion for His disciples. And those
boundaries are clearly defined from the lips of the
Savior as recorded in the New Testament:

> *And I say also unto thee, That thou art
> Peter, and upon this rock I will build my
> church; and the gates of hell shall not pre-
> vail against it.*
> *And I will give unto thee the keys of
> the kingdom of heaven: and whatsoever*

thou shalt bind on earth shall be bound in heaven: and whatsoever thou shalt loose on earth shall be loosed in heaven.

-- Matthew 16:18,19

What are these keys of the kingdom given by our Lord Jesus Christ?

Keys represent authority--dominion.

Peter used the keys of the kingdom when he preached the great prophetic message which inaugurated the birth of the Church and the great thrust of the first group of saints (Acts 2).

Peter further used a key of dominion at the Gate Beautiful of the temple in Jerusalem. A man lame from his mother's womb was brought there daily to beg alms. Then one day things changed for him. As he looked intently upon Peter and John, he heard Peter speak words of dominion, *"In the name of Jesus Christ of Nazareth rise up and walk"* (Acts 3:6).

The Church was not born weak and timid. Strength and dominion opened the new dispensation of grace to the world.

On the housetop of Simon the tanner, Peter received the revelation of world revival and global participation in salvation. With this revelation key he unlocked the prison doors bringing forth the prisoners of the nations. It was the key to world missions.

These keys of the kingdom forever have been and still are in the Church of Jesus Christ. The ministry of binding and loosing belongs to the Church. Whatever is bound on earth shall be bound in heaven. Whatever is loosed on earth shall be loosed in heaven.

The believer's authority on the earth is staggering. Only Deity sets its limits. And heaven backs its God-given dominion.

Chapter 12

EIGHT AREAS OF HUMAN DOMINION

Before proceeding, I wish to emphasize that spiritual dominion is not exclusively a communal or collective power. It is for the individual as well. Many times a person must conquer alone.

In our modern world, the tendency is to identify with large groups. People wish to be associated with big organizations. Even in modern warfare, men who fight may never see the enemy. Their guns and bombs are long range.

But the spiritual battle remains one for the individual. To win in this battle, you personally must exercise dominion.

There was a time in military history when men fought battles as individuals. They won glory for fighting alone. For example, with only the jawbone of an ass, Samson slew a thousand of the enemies of Israel. Young David had a startling confrontation with the giant Goliath. Knowing the power of spiritual dominion, he slew the screaming heavily armed antagonist, with a smooth stone from his slingshot.

When you see that your personal conflict must be a personal victory, you are a long way toward dominion.

Now--where can dominion be taken? And how should dominion be used? Here are eight areas in which you can and should exercise your Christ-given dominion.

1. The World of Transgression--Sin. Take dominion over sin. You do not have to be a slave to sin. You do not have to yield to temptation.

> *For sin shall not have dominion over you: for ye are not under the law, but under grace.*
>
> -- Romans 6:14

Stand upon that promise. Right in the face of temptation, say out loud, "Sin shall not have dominion over me. I dominate in this situation. I choose to dominate over this temptation. I have dominion over sin according to the Word of God."

The longest chapter in the Bible, Psalm 119, is entirely about the Word of God. In the 133rd verse it is recorded that David prayed:

> *Order my steps in thy word: and let not any iniquity have dominion over me.*
>
> -- Psalm 119:133

Make God's Word a part of your very being. Walk according to His Word. Then your steps will be order-ed of the Lord, and you will be invested with might and authority.

2. *The World of Finance--The World of Business.* God wants His people to have the attitude of Adam toward this world. He made everything for Adam. He gave Adam the position of dominion over everything God created. And God created the wealth of the world. The silver and gold are mine, God reminded us in Haggai 2:8.

Abram followed God and became Abraham the blessed. His servant described Abraham's blessings as follows:

> *And he said, I am Abraham's servant.*
> *And the Lord hath blessed my master greatly; and he is become great: and he hath given him flocks, and herds, and silver, and gold, and menservants, and maid-servants, and camels, and asses.*
>
> -- Genesis 24:34,35

The Bible says that he was very rich in cattle, in silver, and in gold (Genesis 13:2). He was a prosper-ous businessman.

But Abraham dominated his riches. They did not dominate him.

His riches did not drive him to strife. When the

You Hold The Reins

land could not support the herds of both Abraham and his nephew, Lot, because *"their substance was great,"* Abraham gave Lot first choice of grazing land, saying, *"Let there be no strife. . . ."* (Genesis 13:5-9). Abraham was not selfish.

Abraham knew that God was the source of his riches (Genesis 14:21-23).

And Abraham paid tithes of all (Genesis 14:20).

The New Testament declares that we which are of faith are the children of Abraham (Galatians 3:9,13, 14,29). Part of that blessing includes financial prosperity and dominion.

God's people should dominate their personal finances and not be dominated by them. We are to exercise responsibility over the financial resources it requires to reach the world with the good news of the kingdom.

3. The Nether World of Demons. Dominion over devils is one of the greatest areas in which a Christian can have power. Divine authority for the child of God extends to a realm which is unseen by the natural man.

Every disciple must know that his warfare is not physical, natural, or carnal. Paul said in Ephesians 6:12, *"For we wrestle not against flesh and blood, but against principalities, against powers, against the rulers of the darkness of this world, against spiritual wickedness in high places."*

Your battle is in the spiritual world. You do not fight flesh and blood, that is, against humans. Your

108

warfare is against the rulers of the darkness of this world. You must pull down the strongholds in high places.

The whole Christian community must recognize an aggressive warfare is being waged on all fronts by unseen and formidable foes. The Church must exercise dominion over the powers of the spiritual world in order to reach the masses of this generation for Christ.

Christ's disciples must do what Mark 16:17 says, *"And these signs shall follow them that believe; In my name shall they cast out devils."*

Who are these devils? They are fallen angels who fell from heaven when Lucifer exalted himself. (See Isaiah 14:12-17; Ezekiel 28:11-19.) These fallen spirits are in complete obedience to their master, Satan. Their job is to dominate humans, to cause them to rebel against God, to corrupt their thoughts, to ruin their lives, and ultimately to cause them to miss Heaven.

It is amazing to me that the heathen, in many instances, are more aware of this world of spirits than many Christians. This very ignorance places the disciple in a losing position in the battle of the spirit world. He must know his enemy in order to defeat him.

The ultimate success or failure of the disciple will not be in the visible world but in the invisible. Just as science at this moment has moved its major activities to outer space, the Church must move its major activities to battle in the heavenlies against the prince and power of the air.

The New Testament sets the divine pattern of dominion over devils. The apostles set men and women free and wrought tremendous victories for the kingdom of God. It must be the same today. Wherever and whenever a possessed person comes in contact with the Spirit-filled disciple, there must be an instantaneous battle for deliverance. If not, the evil spirit will always openly mock the disciple.

The Lord Jesus Christ has given you authority, which is the right to command. He also has given you power, which is the right to act. May you never fail to use this delegated dominion to set men and women free by His power.

You can rejoice in the fact that the day is coming when the devil shall be bound. The Apostle John said in Revelation 20:1-3, *"And I saw an angel come down from heaven, having the key of the bottomless pit and a great chain in his hand. And he laid hold on the dragon, that old serpent, which is the Devil, and Satan, and bound him a thousand years. And cast him into the bottomless pit, and shut him up, and set a seal upon him, that he should deceive the nations no more, till the thousand years should be fulfilled: and after that he must be loosed a little season."*

What a glorious hour it will be when there will be no devil, and because of that, no sin and no sickness. But until that hour, use your Christ-given dominion to paralyze him in every confrontation.

4. The World of Thoughts. The human mind may be the greatest arena of battle in spiritual conflict.

> *For the weapons of our warfare are not carnal, but mighty through God to the pulling down of strong holds;*
>
> *Casting down imaginations, and every high thing that exalteth itself against the knowledge of God, and bringing into captivity EVERY THOUGHT to the obedience of Christ.*
>
> -- 2 Corinthians 10:4,5

Dominion for the disciple includes bringing every thought into captivity and making it obedient to Christ. Every thought is to be controlled and lined up with the Word of God.

When Satan injects thoughts of doubt or fear, they are to be brought into captivity and cast out with the Word of God.

For example, when he tempts you to fear, just stop and say, *"It is written, God has not given us the spirit of fear; but of power, and of love, and of a sound mind"* (2 Timothy 1:7).

A fearful mind is not a sound mind. Rebuke fearful thoughts. A doubtful mind is not a sound mind. Cast out doubts with the Word of Christ.

Also, our minds are not to be garbage containers. If they are, it will be manifested in words and deeds.

111

Do not entertain evil thoughts. The devil may inject one into your mind. Do not allow it to stay. Do not pet it and toy with it. Cast it out immediately and replace it with a thought that meets all these scriptural criteria:

> *Finally, brethren, whatsoever things are*
> *TRUE, whatsoever things are HONEST,*
> *whatsoever things are JUST, whatsoever*
> *things are PURE, whatsoever things are*
> *LOVELY, whatsoever things are of GOOD*
> *REPORT; if there be any virtue, and if*
> *there be any praise, think on these things.*
> -- Philippians 4:8

If a thought is not true, honest, just, pure, lovely, and of good report--simply refuse to allow it to stay in your mind.

This is an area where every disciple can and must assert dominion, thus bringing into captivity every wild and unspiritual thought.

5. *The World of Health and Healing.* Sickness can be made to become obedient to the word of power and authority. In the Great Commission Jesus said, *"These signs shall follow them that believe; In my name . . . they shall lay hands on the sick, and they shall recover"* (Mark 16:17,18).

Centuries earlier God declared that sickness is a curse (Deuteronomy 28:15,22,27,28,35,59-61). So many Christians do not realize this. Some even think

112

that it can be a blessing in certain cases. But God calls it a curse. It is a curse which follows the broken law.

Were it not for Jesus Christ, we would certainly come under this curse with no hope of dominion over sickness. But because of God's great plan of redemption, we are redeemed from the curse of the law, including the curse of sickness:

> *Christ hath redeemed us from the curse of the law, being made a curse for us: for it is written, Cursed is every one that hangeth on a tree.*
>
> -- Galatians 3:13

When Jesus was offered on Calvary's tree as the supreme sacrifice for man's sin, the veil of the temple sectioning off the holy of holies was rent in two from top to bottom. God never again dwelled in temples made with human hands.

In this dispensation of grace, every believer is actually the temple of God. Through the power of the Holy Spirit, God's glorious presence now inhabits a living temple (John 14:23; 1 Corinthians 3:16; 2 Corinthians 6:16).

If God was particular about every detail of His dwelling place in the Old Testament, how much more is He concerned about the living temples for whom Christ died!

> *What? know ye not that your body is the temple of the Holy Ghost which is in you, which ye have of God, and ye are not your own?*
>
> *For ye are bought with a price: therefore glorify God in your body, and in your spirit, which are God's.*
>
> -- 1 Corinthians 6:19,20

It glorifies God for you to have dominion over sickness and disease in your body.

Satan is the author of sickness. Adam knew no sickness until he gave Satan the authority to enter the world with all of his evil merchandise--sin, death, sickness and disease, fear, poverty, lies, and so forth.

Today, in the area of disease, there is authority and counterauthority. The devil has power, as he did with Job, to bring disease upon you. But as a Christian, you possess divine authorization to rebuke, renounce, and destroy all the power of the enemy.

You must exercise your rights, however. Sickness and disease don't just automatically stay away from every believer.

Quote the source of your power. Just as a policeman says, "In the name of the law, stop!" you as Christ's disciple must say, "In Jesus' name, I am healed!"

God promised that none of the diseases of Egypt would come upon His people (Exodus 15:26). Then He revealed Himself as Jehovah-Rapha--"I am the

Lord thy physician," or, "I am the Lord that healeth thee."

The Old Testament is profuse with promises and provision of God's healing power.

Then Jesus came into the world to destroy the works of the devil--including sickness.

> *For this purpose the Son of God was mani-*
> *fested, that he might destroy the works of*
> *the devil.*
>
> *-- 1 John 3:8*

> *Behold, I give unto you power to tread on*
> *serpents and scorpions, and over all the*
> *power of the enemy: and nothing shall by*
> *any means hurt you.*
>
> *-- Luke 10:19*

> *Resist the devil, and he will flee from you.*
> *-- James 4:7*

Christians who are not grounded in the Word are not aware of their dominion in such a strategic area. They do not know that they have the authority to resist the devil and the works of the devil.

I find that the devil is an expert in fifth-column tactics. He sneaks in unaware. He comes in with camouflage. He is a deceiver. He convinces man of his (the devil's) power, and by this creates fears, phobias, confusion, and a feeling of helplessness.

Man receives these terrible things not because the devil cannot be overcome, but because he listens to the devil's voice.

6. The World of Sex. The Bible has much to say about this union between a man and a woman. God performed the first wedding ceremony uniting Adam and Eve. He told them to be fruitful, and multiply, and replenish the earth. In this way, God permitted man to join Him in divinity and in the mystery of life. Life is the greatest mystery in our world. Many mysteries surround mankind, but the greatest is how two protoplasmic cells unite and generate life.

Sex is the most intimate relationship between humans. And only the sexual relationship has the potential of creating an immortal soul. So, from the beginning, God has been very protective about sex. He addressed Himself to it very clearly in His Word. God's moral nature has never altered. He does not change His moral standards to suit a profligate generation.

Since the Garden, Satan has sought to degrade God's creation, man, in the area of sex. All forms of perversion, homosexuality, and moral uncleanness are contrary to God's laws of nature.

The man or woman who does not exercise dominion in the area of sex cannot dominate in any area. They are dominated. They are the victims of frustrations, condemnations, regrets, mental depressions, and physical woes.

God sets people free from all abnormalities and

moral bondage. The person of dominion walks free in this area.

7. *The World of Family.* As we have just seen, God ordained the family. From the first, he intended mankind to exercise authority in their homes. The Garden of Eden was Adam's home. He was told to dress and guard it. He should not have allowed Satan entry into his home. He had the authority to keep him out.

We have the authority to keep the devil out of our gardens. Take the name of Jesus and the sword of the Spirit and put him on the run every time you sense his ugly head appearing. He has to flee.

If you have young children, or plan to have them, determine to train them up in the way they should go. God chose Abraham because He knew he would teach his children. Many fine young families today are bringing up their children from babyhood on the milk of God's Word. They speak of the Lord in their homes at all times.

Perhaps your children are older. And maybe they were into trouble before you became knowledgeable in the things of God. God's Word says that children are a blessing from the Lord. Claim that promise. Take the name of Jesus and break the power of the devil over your children--then claim them for Jesus Christ. Look at them in faith and love.

Your home is to be a haven of peace and love. Discipline yourself to walk in love there. Walk in the 13th chapter of First Corinthians and you will walk in dominion in your family life.

8. Dominion in the World to Come. We shall be kings and priests forever! Christian dominion by the blood of the Lord Jesus Christ is not only meant for this life, but the Word of God teaches that we will carry dominion into the world beyond.

> *And the kingdom and dominion, and the greatness of the kingdom under the whole heaven, shall be given to the people of the saints of the most High, whose kingdom is an everlasting kingdom, and all dominions shall serve and obey him.*
>
> -- Daniel 7:27

Kingdoms and dominion will be given to the victorious saints. And this shall be world without end.

> *And from Jesus Christ, who is the faithful witness, and the first begotten of the dead, and the prince of the kings of the earth. Unto him that loved us, and washed us from our sins in his own blood,*
> *And hath made us kings and priests unto God and his Father; to him be glory and dominion for ever and ever. Amen.*
>
> -- Revelation 1:5,6

In the future life, the victorious disciple is to be a king and a priest. This dominion includes the material realm as well as the spiritual. It also signifies serving

and being served, a peculiar and glorious combination
of servant and lord.

Chapter 13

POWER
AGAINST POWER

We live in a generation today which could be defined as a power generation.

We have power drugs--sometimes used the wrong way.

We have power machines--new ones are developed every year.

We have power politics--you'd better believe it.

The world is drunk on power--dominion. Man loves power, from the popping of an inch-long firecracker to the blasting of an atomic bomb. Almost the total world is seeking greater power.

Inside the earth we look for coal--hidden power which has lain dormant for centuries. We bring it out and transform it into power to move engines and heat furnaces.

Deep into the bowels of the earth we drive machinery to suck out oil and gas for our mechanized age.

Electricity is power. Daily the world searches for new ways to make it. Our society is dependent on power through electricity.

When man took hold of atomic power to harness and release it, he touched something theretofore untouched by human hands. In Japan, two cities disintegrated. They melted by the forces of atomic bombs. Since that day, the world has feared that they might fall again.

In the air above us, radio waves speed around the world at 180,000 miles per second. That's seven times around the world in one second!

At our television station here in South Bend, Indiana, we have a link-up with a satellite. A television broadcast image can leave Virginia or North Carolina or California--or any other place which is producing an up-link--travel 22,300 miles above the earth to the satellite and back down through the down-link in South Bend in less than a second. You can barely bat your eye before it is up and back down again.

Yes, our world is power conscious. Almost everyone in the world is also conscious that power can be used in two ways--constructively or destructively. Man has to decide which way to use power.

The Power of Sin

There is· a power that destroys. The power of sin is the greatest destroyer of all mankind.

Organized crime--an evil which has hurt multitudes

of people--operates through the power of sin.

Men are murderers through the power of sin. It is almost sickening to listen to any newscast. They are replete with reports of murders in small hamlets and large cities--men killing men, women killing women, children killing children. Mankind seems to have lost the thing God gave us--respect for human life and human dignity.

Sin causes all murders. Sin causes all thefts. Sin causes all adultery. Sin causes all drunkenness, all gambling, all cheating. All moral uncleanness comes from sin. Sin is to blame for all of it. Sin is a monster. It has power.

No human can tackle the power of sin and win over it. Your human power cannot stand up against sin's power. The reason is, the devil is the originator of sin. He is the head captain of all that steals, kills, or destroys.

> *The thief cometh not, but for to steal, and to kill, and to destroy. . . .*
> -- John 10:10

Natural human strength is no match for Satan's power.

The Bible describes his person in his original state. In Heaven he was *"full of wisdom, and perfect in beauty"* (Ezekiel 28:12). He was covered with every perfect stone that glitters--diamonds, rubies, and other precious stones adorned him (v. 13).

122

But Lucifer turned his God-given will against God. The will he was to have used to choose to worship God, he turned against his Creator. He rebelled against God, and he fell from his place of beauty and glory. Isaiah 14:12-15 tells the terrible story.

Jesus told his disciples how he had beheld Satan as lightning fall from Heaven (Luke 10:18).

Isaiah 14:12 identifies him as the one who weakened the nations. Every nation that becomes weak is weakened by his power. He is the destroyer of nations.

He is described as the one who made the earth to tremble (Isaiah 14:16). Every time there is a war, revolution, or turmoil, down beneath it all, the devil is there. He shakes kingdoms (v. 16).

He made the world a wilderness, and destroyed the cities thereof (v. 17). I went to Europe just a few days after World War II was over. In London I saw buildings I had lived in completely destroyed. The Bible college I had preached in was gone. In France whole cities where I had preached many times were nothing but rubble. I just stood there and cried, "Oh, God! Oh, God!" Any time you see destruction, there is a sinister personality close by--the devil. His ministry is one of destruction.

The Power of Our Savior

Now let's look at the other side of the calendar. God's Word tells us of a *far greater power:*

*But we preach Christ crucified, unto the
Jews a stumblingblock, and unto the
Greeks foolishness;*
But unto them which are called, both
Jews and Greeks, CHRIST THE POWER
OF GOD, AND THE WISDOM OF GOD.
-- 1 Corinthians 1:23,24

What is Christ? Christ is the power of God!

*For I am not ashamed of THE GOSPEL OF
CHRIST: for it IS THE POWER OF GOD
unto salvation to every one that believeth. . . .*
-- Romans 1:16

Jesus is the power of God. And the Gospel is the
power of God. The Gospel we preach is not words,
not notions, not philosophic ideas--it is the power of
God!

*But as many as received him, to them gave
he POWER to become the sons of God,
even to them that believe on his name.*
-- John 1:12

When we receive Christ into our hearts, something
happens to us. To as many as receive Him, He gives
power!

124

But ye shall receive POWER,after that the Holy Ghost is come upon you: and ye shall be witnesses unto me both in Jerusalem, and in all Judaea, and in Samaria, and unto the uttermost part of the earth.

-- Acts 1:8

Here is additional power! Additional strength! We receive power after the Holy Ghost is come upon us. Aren't you glad for that?

When I think of power against power, it reminds me of a dam. To stop a river from running, you dam it up and make a lake out of it. A point of decision must be reached. Which is stronger--the water flowing down the river, or the dam? Usually, because the dam has been conceived and engineered by brilliant minds, it can stand all the water. Waves beat against it, flood waters rise against it, but the dam just stays there. Its staying power is stronger than the coming power-- so the coming power can do nothing but back off.

When it is power against power, the weaker power must back off. When it is power against power, one power will always supersede.

God's power will always supersede the power of evil when we exercise it. God wants to bring His children to the place where we know and exercise our God-given power.

When Satan comes against God's people, he should find a dam stretched across saying, "Come on, waters of evil, we're here to stay. We're here to hold you back. We're here to circumscribe you--to tell you how far you can go."

Steel is tough. And they can make it tougher and tougher. They can get it so tough that steel won't cut steel. But there is something called a diamond. Just a little diamond put into a vice can be brought against steel to cut it.

Why? It's force against force--power against power. Something has to give.

The steel says, "I am tough."

The diamond says, "Yes, but I am tougher. You yield to me. Yield to me any way I want you to yield. I want you to know I am the boss."

Jesus was talking about power against power when He said, *"But if I cast out devils by the Spirit of God, then the kingdom of God is come unto you. Or else how can one enter into a strong man's house, and spoil his goods, except he first bind the strong man? and then he will spoil his house"* (Matthew 12:28,29).

The devil may be tough, but we are tougher. He may be strong, but we are stronger. We have to know this, however. We have to live like this. We must live with the power of God today. We must live with the divine authority of God.

A friend I met in Indonesia some years ago has always been an inspiration to me. She was a little Dutch missionary from Holland.

She went back into the mountains of Indonesia and was preaching there when the local witch doctor told her to leave. He said she was in his territory.

She said, "You don't have any territory. I am going to stay."

He said, "No! I don't like other witch doctors coming in here. I respect other witch doctors. I don't go into their places and I don't want them in mine."

She said, "I'm no witch doctor."

He said, "You act like one."

They quarrelled for some time. Finally, the witch doctor said, "I am willing to do something. Let's see who has the most power. The one who has less power, let that one leave."

The missionary agreed.

The witch doctor said, "Let's meet on a certain day and ask everybody to come."

On that certain day, everyone was there. They thought two witch doctors were going to have a contest to see who would be boss of that community.

Just the two of them--the young woman missionary and the witch doctor--stepped up onto the platform.

The witch doctor looked at her and said, "Do something."

She didn't know what to do, so she said, "You do something."

He did! He lay down on the floor before all the people. Then he went stiff as a board. Very slowly, the powers of levitation caught him. He rose up ankle high, then knee high, where he floated in the air.

The people were beside themselves. Surely he was the most powerful, they said.

The Dutch girl thought, <u>I know I can't float. I
guess I'll have to leave.</u>

God said, "No, you don't!"

She said, "Well, what am I going to do?"

God said, "Get him down! Put your foot in his
belly and push him down."

So she walked over to him, pulled up her long
skirt a little, put her foot in his belly, and pushed
him against the floor.

Then God said, "Cast the devil out of him!"

So she said, "Come out of him!!!"

The devil came out at her command. And when
the man came to his senses, he didn't know where he
was. He was so full of the devil he hadn't been in his
right mind. He didn't even know the contest was
taking place.

He said, "Where am I? What am I doing here?
What is this all about?"

She reached over and pulled him up to a seated
position. She told him what had happened, and he
received Jesus as his Savior. She laid hands on him
and he received the Holy Spirit.

When I arrived there, that community had let
the whole island know that if anybody who'd received Jesus was being persecuted, they could come
there and live with them. They called the community
the Refugee Town.

The missionary was the administrator. The former
witch doctor was the mayor. When they had a community meeting, she sat in a chair and he sat in a

chair. As long as things went all right, she didn't say a word. When they needed a little help, she went at it. They worked together now. But that day they met on the platform, it was power against power.

In our everyday lives we face things--not exactly like that confrontation--but just as surely power against power. It is up to us to decide who is the winner.

Jesus Christ is the winner. God wants each of us to be winners, too. He has made the provision for us always to triumph in Christ Jesus. He wants every one of us to know His mighty power. He wants every one of us to confess His mighty power. You cannot confess defeat and give Jesus right of way in your life. You must confess victory in Jesus' name.

Yes, until the end of this age it will always be power against power. But God's Word has settled forever the fact that the greater power resides in the believer.

> *Ye are of God, little children, and have overcome them: because GREATER IS HE THAT IS IN YOU, THAN HE THAT IS IN THE WORLD.*　　-- 1 John 4:4

The "them" we "have overcome" are demons and evil spirits. The Greater One who is in us is Jesus through the power of the Holy Spirit. The devil is "he that is in the world."

Jesus is the Greater One. He is in us. We are not losers. We are winners. We have God's power!

129

Chapter 14

YOU HOLD THE REINS

One of my greatest thrills as a boy was the first time I held the reins to a team of prancing, dancing horses as they pulled a wagon. To drive an automobile for the first time has no thrill like feeling the flesh and blood of spirited steeds, ready to obey your every wish as you pull upon the reins.

But the greatest thrill of liberation and dominion in the world is to sense the vibrant life of Christ flooding your spirit, your mind, and your body, making you free from every tormenting habit, phobia, and fear.

You feel that God has handed you the reins of the universe and said, "Drive on victoriously through this life to the City of God." That's Dominion!

Jesus is now handing you the reins of your destiny and saying, "You hold the reins!"

Take them. Don't be dependent upon others any longer. What a thrill it is to experience the joy and confidence of knowing that you hold the reins of human life and you are guiding your own destiny. You are not under the power of any demon, or disease, or doctrine, or denomination, but you are free and ready to drive on furiously and gloriously to untold victories by the power and authority given you by the Lord Jesus Christ.

Dependency on Others

In our modern world, millions of people are almost totally dependent on others for their very lives. Many must always have an evangelist or pastor support and strengthen them by prayer for physical and spiritual debilitation. Many seek out specialists to pry deep into their consciences searching for solutions to deep-rooted problems. They lean on psychologists or psychiatrists to help them out of mental confusion. Some need pep pills to get going in the morning and tranquilizers to calm their troubled nerves at night. These people never have known the joy nor the confidence that comes with holding the reins of life--to get up feeling good and retire feeling fulfilled.

Victories won by someone else can be lost by one's own weakness later. Healings wrought by another's prayers can be lost in a moment of defeat at home or work. To realize real victory and keep healing, one must learn that Jesus Christ will do for him personally all that He will do for anyone else at any time or any place.

No one will be completely free or permanently healed until he personally learns how to stay free by God's power.

We must hold the reins of our lives in our own hands.

"Woman, You Take the Reins"

Two women drove eleven hundred miles, one way, for me to say a prayer for one of them. She had been institutionalized.

After praying a prayer of deliverance over this woman, and observing the glory of God come upon her, and seeing the smile of relief come into her face, and hearing her pray a prayer of deliverance and giving thanks to God, I said to her, "Now, you can take the reins and drive! You are in command! You hold the reins of your destiny. You can stay free by your own prayers and God's power. However, you must exercise a spiritual determination to be free and realize that YOU now hold the reins! You do not have to return to me--Jesus is the same to you as He is to me."

She became vibrant with a new hope. Her eyes, which had looked glassy, suddenly became alert. She realized for the first time in her life that she was now the master of her own destiny. I could just picture her driving a Roman chariot with dashing horses moving ahead at great speed while she held the reins calm and secure!

Half-Delivered

I am certain there are multitudes of people who are only half-blessed and half-healed because they have not been taught the full truth.

It is not enough to come to the altar and say, "Lord, forgive me of my sins." The sins would be gone, but the person's inner being still would be empty. Full salvation comes when one lifts his heart to God and becomes filled with His love, His joy, His peace, and with His total salvation.

It is not sufficient for a demon possessed person only to become dispossessed. Once people are delivered by the strength of Christ, they must become filled with His Spirit. Then they must take the reins of power and authority in their own hands under their Lord's direction.

If they will do that, they are virtually unlimited in the heights they can ascend.

You Are Unlimited

As a man thinketh in his heart, so is he.
                                             -- Proverbs 23:7

Only God sets the limits for those in divine relationship with Him. He says we are unlimited if we can think right and believe right in our hearts. Everything Heaven has is open to any one of us who meets God's requirements. But we must go after it. Blessing and power will not be handed to us.

How often we hear of some especially blessed person, "He's a lucky guy," or "She's a lucky person." That's untrue. We do not accept the false claims of luck. Every successful person I ever knew did everything he could to work with God.

The small boy with the five loaves and two fishes became unlimited when he handed them to Jesus. The Apostle Peter became unlimited when he stepped out of the boat onto the tempestuous waves!

Unlimited Concepts

When you hold the reins of your own life, you are limited only by your conception of what you can do. If you deeply believe you can do something, that is half the battle.

Many limit themselves through wrong thinking, then become the victims of their own limitations.

What you can accomplish does not depend upon your abilities and talents. You may say you are not naturally able to do this or that, but with God, you can become unlimited.

What you can accomplish does not depend upon what you are naturally. It does not depend upon your abilities and talents. You may say you are not naturally able to do this or that, but with God, you can become unlimited.

Unlimited Worship

The living, vibrant, glorious Church is unlimited.

Remember, Jesus said the gates of hell could not prevail against it. Only the individual members who make up the Body of Christ limit the activities and victories of the Church. The Church is what we make it to be--what we believe it to be. We could say, "As the Church thinks in its heart, so is it."

As an individual member of the universal Church, you will help the Body of Christ in the earth to complete its ministry by taking your place as a free and victorious "member in particular."

Unlimited Relationships

We are unlimited in our relationship to God. No one has reached the maximum possible in God. No one has climbed the ultimate heights. What a challenge stands before us. Inside me I am looking up to God as if I were a young beginning minister. I know there is still a world to save.

Your personal relationship to God is unlimited. You can be what you want to be. You can reach out for God's highest and best. God will call your name and say to you, "You can have anything you can conceive in your heart. Conceive it and you can have it." It takes time in God's presence in meditation and prayer to get God's best. But if you are willing to do it--and you hold the reins of your life, no power holds you back--you are unlimited in your relationship with God.

It is challenging to reach higher than you have ever

before reached. And remember, God is not limited to your weakness or frailty. If He can take a Jacob and make an Israel out of him, He can do something big for you. I challenge you--be unlimited in your relationship to God.

Further, you are unlimited in your relationship with your fellow man. You are unlimited in the quantity and quality of your friends.

Perhaps you don't realize it, but you have the number of friends you desire. You have the number of friends you went out to get. If you don't have many friends, you didn't go out to get many. You might have thought they were the deciding factor. That's wrong. You are the deciding factor.

You can win anybody you want for a friend. If you don't have enough friends, get busy! Be nice to about forty people and you will be amazed how it works! Be unselfish. Do a little something extra for somebody and you will be amazed at how well you are liked.

Practice smiling a little more. I've noticed that sometimes as people grow older, they get a little too sober. Problems come, but we're not slaves of problems.

You are unlimited in your greatest treasure on this earth--your friends. They come at the right time. They say the right word with the right touch. Friends are more to be desired than any thing on the earth.

People who have no friends are miserable. People

who have many friends are the happiest people in the world! Be a true friend to many people.

Unlimited Health

I believe that health is a state of spirit--a state of the inner man. When we say within us, "I have health. I have life. I have vitality in Jesus' name," I think we already have made three fourths of the journey toward health.

But when we say we are sick, then we are sick. If we say, "Well, you know my grandpa was always sick. I'm going to be sick, too," whether we are sick or not, we get sick.

Accept health unlimited. Look up to the sky and say, "My life must shine as the stars. My life must be as beautiful and fragrant as the flowers." Look at all of God's work and say, "I will be like the rest of God's kingdom. I will be well and strong and happy." You will be unlimited in health and strength.

Remember, God's Word says, *"As a man thinketh in his heart. . . ."* Our faith has to do with our health.

Unlimited Prosperity

Christians are unlimited in prosperity. God blesses those who serve Him--Christian nations or individual followers of Christ. God prospers those who recognize His power to supply all needs.

Some Christians who had little opportunity for education became mighty in the world of business. They discovered the secret in Christ of being unlimited.

It is disturbing to me when people speak with the limitations of unbelief. I believe our God can do anything. If great things don't happen, don't blame God. Start searching within asking God what you can do to be unlimited. Let God's people be like the eagle when he stretches his powerful wings and flies into the sky screaming, "Unlimited! Unlimited!" The great open heavens are his home. It is unlimited up there.

You can take the reins of your life and move into God and into areas of unlimited blessing, unlimited anointing, unlimited faith, unlimited victory, unlimited success, unlimited friendship, unlimited prosperity.

The whole world stands before you, and you have the key. Don't lock the door--open it and march forward!

But don't be selfish. If a person reaches into the unlimited resources of God for selfish purposes, it is wrong. Do it to help others, to love others, and to bless others, and God will grant you the desires of your heart.

Stay free! Stay victorious! And stay unlimited! Reach for the unlimited heights for Jesus' sake, for the sake of others, and for happiness within yourself.

I don't know about you, but I am only happy in victory. I am never happy in defeat. When a friend is victorious, I am happy in his victory. When another is anointed, I am happy in his anointing.

You are the only one who can limit your life. Don't do it. Get ready for the blessings to flow. Say, "Lord, let them flow." Then command them to flow unlimitedly!

Release your total being to the unlimited God--and know the true meaning of life in the Spirit.

Write today
for your free catalog
of LESEA materials available:

LESEA Ministries
P.O. Box 12
South Bend, IN 46624

Lester Sumrall, President